THE MATHS AND DYSCALCULIA ASSESSMENT

from the author

Understanding Dyscalculia and Numeracy Difficulties
A Guide for Parents, Teachers and Other Professionals
Patricia Babtie and Jane Emerson
ISBN 978 1 84905 390 7
eISBN 978 0 85700 754 4

The MATHS and DYSCALCULIA ASSESSMENT

Jane Emerson and **Robert Jennings**

Jessica Kingsley Publishers
London and Philadelphia

First published in Great Britain in 2025 by Jessica Kingsley Publishers
An imprint of John Murray Press

1

Copyright © Jane Emerson and Robert Jennings 2025

The right of Jane Emerson and Robert Jennings to be identified as the Author of the Work has been asserted by them in accordance with the Copyright, Designs and Patents Act 1988.

The Dyscalculia Checklist © The Dyscalculia Network 2025
Illustrations © Joseph Latham 2025

Front cover image source: Shutterstock®.

All rights reserved. No part of this publication may be reproduced, stored in a retrieval system, or transmitted, in any form or by any means without the prior written permission of the publisher, nor be otherwise circulated in any form of binding or cover other than that in which it is published and without a similar condition being imposed on the subsequent purchaser.

All pages marked ⇩ may be downloaded for personal use with this programme, but may not be reproduced for any other purposes without the permission of the publisher.

A CIP catalogue record for this title is available from the British Library and the Library of Congress

ISBN 978 1 80501 175 0
eISBN 978 1 80501 176 7

Printed and bound by CPI Group (UK) Ltd, Croydon, CR0 4YY

Jessica Kingsley Publishers' policy is to use papers that are natural, renewable and recyclable products and made from wood grown in sustainable forests. The logging and manufacturing processes are expected to conform to the environmental regulations of the country of origin.

Jessica Kingsley Publishers
Carmelite House
50 Victoria Embankment
London EC4Y 0DZ

www.jkp.com

John Murray Press
Part of Hodder & Stoughton Limited
An Hachette UK Company

The authorised representative in the EEA is Hachette Ireland,
8 Castlecourt Centre, Dublin 15, D15 XTP3, Ireland (email: info@hbgi.ie)

Contents

Acknowledgements	7
Foreword by Dr Steve Chinn	8
Preface	9
Introduction to the Maths and Dyscalculia Assessment (MDA)	**10**
What you will find in this manual and test kit	10
How to use the MDA and the benefits of using it	11
What's unique about the MDA?	12
How the book is structured	12

PART 1: What Are Dyscalculia and Maths Difficulties and How Do We Screen and Test for Them? — 15

1. An Introduction to Dyscalculia and Maths Difficulties	**16**
Background: How common are dyscalculia and maths learning difficulties?	16
A new dyscalculia definition?	17
The nature of maths learning	19
Other causes of difficulties with maths	20
Maths anxiety	22
2. Indicators of Maths Difficulties and a Checklist	**27**
3. Maths Screeners	**32**

PART 2: Guide to Using the Maths and Dyscalculia Assessment — 35

4. Getting Started	**36**
Getting organized	36
What's in the test?	37
Environment/room preparation	39
First impressions	40
Timing	40
Recording answers and techniques used	41

5. A Step-by-Step Guide to Administering the Test   43
Starting out   43
General principles   43
Using the detailed section explanations in this chapter   44

    Section A – Number Sense   46
    Section B – Counting   47
    Section C – Sequencing   48
    Section D – Writing and Reading Numbers   50
    Section E – Early Calculation   51
    Section F – Doubles/Halves   53
    Section G – Components of Numbers   54
    Section H – Number Bonds for 10 and Above   55
    Section I – Place Value   57
    Section J – Addition   59
    Section K – Subtraction   61
    Section L – Multiplication   63
    Section M – Division   66
    Section N – Word Problems   68
    Section O – Fractions   69
    Section P – Decimals   72
    Section Q – Percentages   73
    Section R – Measurement   74
    Section S – Conversions   75

6. Interpreting the Results   77
Error analysis: Looking at student errors   77

7. Developing a Teaching Intervention Plan   109
Example of an assessment using the MDA   112
Reassessment   112

Conclusion   116

PART 3: Appendices   117

Appendix A: *Summary Report and Teaching Plan Template and Example*   118
Appendix B: *Blank Family Questionnaire*   121
Appendix C: *Useful Websites with Resources for Teachers and Parents*   129

Bibliography   131
About the Authors   133

Acknowledgements

First, we thank the late Dorian Yeo, who pioneered and developed a new approach to teaching numeracy at Emerson House, London. Professor Emeritus Brian Butterworth and Professor Diana Laurillard have also supported this approach to maths teaching over the years and provided important insights into the approaches used, particularly with the assessment of dyscalculia and targeted online games using dice and the new dot patterns up to 10.

Catherine Eadle, co-founder of The Dyscalculia Network, has been inspirational and supportive in assisting with testing and providing advice on this new assessment. Rebecca Thompson has provided help in understanding the definition of dyscalculia and SpLD in mathematics.

Joe Latham has delivered some really excellent illustrations, which represent the nature and purpose of this book.

We have all been inspired by the important work of Dr Steve Chinn at the school he founded, Mark College; he continues to provide valuable input.

Next, we look back to and thank the teachers, past and present, at Emerson House, who have supported the development of *The Maths and Dyscalculia Assessment* with their insights. In particular, we acknowledge the support and encouragement of Cathryn Learoyd, Principal.

We also remember all the children who have taught us so much over the years by being willing to talk about their understanding and difficulties with their maths, which led to our greater understanding of their different strengths and weaknesses.

Jane Emerson and Robert Jennings

Foreword

I am delighted to have been asked to write this foreword for the MDA, *The Maths and Dyscalculia Assessment*, written by Jane Emerson and Rob Jennings, authors whose work I have several connections to.

I firmly believe that the best grounding for understanding students with learning differences is found in the classroom, where one has the chance to watch and listen to the learners as they think through their developing understanding of numeracy. Jane, as a specialist advisor now, and Rob, as an assessor and specialist teacher, are both experienced, skilled and empathetic listeners, and this gives their work a realistic practicality.

The MDA will help teachers and parents to develop appropriate skills for communicating with and teaching students. Research is very important, so that we can gain evidence-based data, but I have seen how empathic classroom experience is even more valuable. These two approaches, applied by Jane and Rob in this tool, will bear the best fruit together.

The MDA informs about the diagnosis of needs. When we use it with learners, it guides the structure of interventions, developed through the analysis of any errors shown in the graded sections. It will help those assisting the students to understand many of the barriers to their learning and to address them and circumvent many of them, with appropriate and accessible approaches.

Many years of working in special needs taught me that often educators are called on to make a strong case for extra provision and for the funding that is involved in this. Detailed data can be most helpful in arguing a case for additional input.

Assessment and diagnosis can be stressful for young people. Gaining a realistic picture can be crucial, and if that process evokes fear and anxiety, clear ways to assist will not be achieved. The MDA is designed to be learner-friendly and to keep maths anxiety in the students to a minimum while identifying their individual learning needs in this important subject. The MDA is also designed to be educationally and financially accessible. It is an impressive achievement.

Dr Steve Chinn

Preface

The Maths and Dyscalculia Assessment is not a standardized test. We have devised it to have an informal structure, detailing a more formative, step-by-step approach that builds on existing knowledge. It will provide the adult assessing the student with information on what the student can and can't do, and why that is the case.

As awareness grows around maths difficulties and we identify increasing numbers of school students (and adults) showing signs of dyscalculia and maths difficulties in schools and in the wider public, the Maths and Dyscalculia Assessment we have created at the Dyscalculia Network is a test that is urgently needed now, to ensure that students with maths difficulties get the right, tailored support that they need with their mathematics learning. We have designed and road-tested this test kit so that you, as a teacher or parent, will be able to find the right teaching interventions that target the student's foundational learning needs in the different areas of their maths learning. As you will see, we also pay attention to wider factors and cognitive differences that all feed into a maths student's profile.

We do plan, over time, to develop the MDA in the future to include standardized scores on both accuracy and time taken to complete each section. The standardization process will evaluate the student's learning compared to agreed standards or benchmarks. We plan to use both formative (providing ongoing feedback for the learner and the teacher) and summative assessments (an evaluation of the learner at the end of the instructional period). In order to ensure the validity and reliability of the assessment's standardization, in due course, we will be using a wide range of test data, which will take some time to collect. We wanted this test to be available now, when the need is there, so that students with maths difficulties and dyscalculia get the support they require as soon as possible. The MDA has been developed over a number of years and has been tested with a wide range of learners. This has enabled us to fine-tune the assessment to include all of the key areas of foundation maths. This enables the teacher or parent to build up a picture of the strengths and weaknesses of the learner and to implement a more focused intervention plan for them.

Introduction to the Maths and Dyscalculia Assessment (MDA)

What you will find in this manual and test kit

The assessment comprises this manual that you are reading and two accompanying test kits, each with an assessor booklet and student booklet, which are downloadable online.

As we state in the Preface, we have designed this test to enable teachers and other adults supporting children and teens (and adult students) with maths difficulties to get the support they need with their maths learning, through a process of identifying their areas of difficulty and where the gaps in their foundational knowledge are.

The MDA is a wide-ranging assessment, which covers all of the main foundation topics of numeracy, which scaffold future maths learning.

- There are 19 sections in each test kit, and each section is explained in the **main manual**, which you are reading now. These cover a number of basic topics such as number sense, counting, sequencing, writing and reading numbers, early calculation, doubles and halves, components of numbers, number bonds for 10 and above, place value, addition, subtraction, multiplication, division, and more advanced topics such as word problems, fractions, decimals, percentages, measurement and conversions.

- The manual guides you in using the two **online test kits**.

- The two online test kits – A (blue) and B (red) – are available as free downloads to purchasers of this book from https://library.jkp.com/redeem, using the code GLPUYJM.

- The two test kits each comprise two parts, an assessor booklet and a student test booklet. The two tests should be used at intervals of no less than six months. This will enable the assessing adult to quantify progress from any targeted interventions they have put in place as a result of doing the first test with the student.

- Each test takes approximately 60 minutes to complete. (This will vary depending upon the individual's maths abilities.)

- The MDA is designed mainly for use by students aged 6–18, although there is no reason why it cannot be used for adults too, if they are seeking understanding of their maths difficulties.

- The MDA allows you as the adult assessor to observe and record key information about what the student says and does as they do maths. This could include the student's use of strategies such as counting, or their existing knowledge, such as number bonds and other strategies for calculations.

- In each student booklet in the respective test kits, there is an informal opening page, for the student to do some free drawing or doodling. While they draw, you can gently encourage them to discuss their general attitude to maths and what they believe they know and understand.

Each of the two tests (A and B) has been designed as two booklets: one for the assessor, to keep scores and notes on the individual, and a separate student booklet for the child or teen being assessed.

How to use the MDA and the benefits of using it

The MDA tool is designed for assessors to use in the following ways:

- It provides you with **statistical data** to back up your observations on all assessed students who are struggling with maths. This includes detailed scores on each section. For example, there are 11 questions in the addition topic, and the scores could be analysed statistically. If you are a parent using this tool, this data will provide you with the necessary detail to discuss with your child's school and demonstrate your child's struggles with maths and their need for specific support and intervention.

- It allows you to specify a **diagnostic analysis** of both strengths and weaknesses of the individual, in order to plan teaching or home-schooling intervention, based upon the results. Teaching should begin at or just before the most basic levels where difficulties are found in the assessment.

- The MDA's **straightforward and easy-to-use** format means that it can be used by educational psychologists, maths or form teachers, specialists trained in teaching students with special education needs, SENCOs and teaching assistants, and home-schooling parents or parents wishing to supplement their children's maths learning.

- The tests in the MDA provide a measurement of **the time the student takes in minutes/seconds** for each section to be completed. This will enable the assessor to measure if the student is taking longer than expected to complete a calculation, even if they achieve a correct answer. This is incredibly useful to know as it can identify when the student is using more rudimentary strategies to reach that correct answer. Intervention might then be provided to support the student to use more developed methods and strategies to get to the answer. For example, a student may be using their fingers and counting up or back in ones. When they have calculations involving larger numbers, they may achieve the correct answer using this method, but it will take them much longer than a more developed strategy.

What's unique about the MDA?

- The maths section of a typical educational assessment may lack the level of detail we provide here in terms of the student's actual maths abilities. The MDA really delves into the maths the student can do and how they approach it. It is uniquely useful in enabling the person doing the assessing to devise an appropriate intervention plan for the student.

- It has a clear and easy-to-use format.

- It allows the assessor an opportunity to understand if there are discrepancies between the student's accuracy in their calculations and their speed of execution.

- The two tests A (blue) and B (red) allow repeat testing after six months, so the assessor can review the student's progress as a result of planned intervention. Progress can therefore be monitored regularly, and you can provide evidence of progress achieved.

How the book is structured

This book is divided into three parts.

The first part looks at what dyscalculia and maths difficulties are and how to screen for them, and provides background information about dyscalculia and maths difficulties and their impact on maths learning. It also discusses maths anxiety and how it needs to be addressed before we can hope to help students acquire mathematical understanding.

The second part of the book provides a step-by-step guide on how to administer the MDA, including how to prepare beforehand and how to record information about the learner being assessed. It has a section-by-section breakdown of the downloadable tests (Test A (blue) and Test B (red)), which are included with the purchase of this book.

The third part of this book provides a guide to interpreting the results from the tests, explains what the errors could indicate and offers guidance on how to develop a teaching intervention plan, including how to create a summary assessment report.

Finally, the Appendices A and B includes two key forms: a Family Questionnaire, which can be used to provide important background information on the student being assessed and the Summary Report and Teaching Plan Template, which you can use when you create a summary assessment report. Appendix C has a list of useful resources for teachers and parents if you want further information, advice or ideas for maths games for dyscalculia and maths difficulties.

PART 1

What Are Dyscalculia and Maths Difficulties and How Do We Screen and Test for Them?

CHAPTER 1
An Introduction to Dyscalculia and Maths Difficulties

Background: How common are dyscalculia and maths learning difficulties?

Research has shown that numeric and arithmetic abilities are equally as important for life success as literacy skills and that difficulties with maths can have severe effects on individuals' wellbeing as well as a nation's economy. Current estimates have shown that approximately 20 per cent of the population in Organisation for Economic Co-operation and Development (OECD) countries have difficulties with mathematics, imposing great practical and occupational restrictions. Around 5–7 per cent of the population have dyscalculia (Vogel and De Smedt 2021).

Yet compared with other special educational learning difficulties, dyscalculia receives limited recognition within the wider education support system and lacks the same level of funding and research interest.

In the UK, Pete Jarrett for the British Dyslexia Association (2022) outlines that between 2010 and 2020, the Welcome Trust funded dyslexia with £3 million and dyscalculia with only £1 million; between 2005 and 2019, UK Research and Innovation funded dyslexia with £107 million and dyscalculia with only £23 million.

In *Dyscalculia: From Science to Education* (2019), cognitive neuropsychologist Professor Brian Butterworth writes that, since 2000, the National Institute of Health in the United States has spent $107.2 million in funding for dyslexia research but only $2.3 million on dyscalculia. This is despite the prevalence of the two conditions being similar.

In a report by the Every Child a Chance Trust/KPMG (Gross, Hudson and Price 2009), the annual economic damage caused by poor numeracy skills in the UK (the lack of skilled labour, public social spending, private insolvency, etc.) was estimated at £2.4 billion, higher than the economic damage caused by dyslexia.

In the final report for the Foresight Mental Capital and Wellbeing Project (2008), developmental dyscalculia (defined in medical terms as a congenital neurological developmental disorder) was estimated to reduce lifetime earnings by £114,000 and reduce the probability of achieving an acceptable pass grade in a public exam by 7–20 percentage points.

In her latest research, Kinga Morsanyi (Senior Lecturer in Mathematical Cognition at Loughborough University) states that: 'A child with Dyscalculia is a hundred times less likely to be diagnosed and to receive educational support than a dyslexic child' (2018).

This discrepancy in research, funding and support shows the importance of the MDA, as this apparent lack of awareness can have consequences for both the individual and the wider community.

Maths is a key skill that you need just to go to the corner shop to buy bread, to split the bill with your friend in a restaurant or to manage your own budgets and finances as an adult. Passing maths GCSE is a requirement for going further in education and failure to do so can act as a barrier to career enhancement. It is incredibly important that students with innate maths difficulties get the right support early on in their lives so they can navigate mathematical content in their later lives with confidence and access the same opportunities as others.

A new dyscalculia definition?

The SpLD Assessment Standards Committee (SASC) is a representative organization for professionally qualified diagnostic assessors of specific learning difficulties (SpLD). SASC members work to agreed standards of practice, established collaboratively by the organization.

In 2025, they have published a new set of guidance on the assessment of mathematics difficulties and dyscalculia. This is based upon the work by the Working Group on Maths Difficulties and Dyscalculia and the new definition is based upon the latest research and thinking. The full document can be found on the SASC Website: https://www.sasc.org.uk/news/maths-difficulties-and-dyscalculia-guidance-march-25.

The new definition has created a **'specific learning difficulty in mathematics (2025)'**, of which dyscalculia is a sub-category.

The new guidelines outline a specific learning difficulty in mathematics as a set of processing difficulties that affects the acquisition of arithmetic and other areas of mathematics.

In the new guidelines, the key markers of an SpLD in mathematics, irrespective of levels of education and different age groups, are difficulties in arithmetic fluency and flexibility as well as mathematical problem solving.

Arithmetic fluency tests generally measure automaticity and often perpetuate the misunderstanding that fluency is all about remembering facts and applying standard procedures. We need to look beyond them and analyse performance in additional ways, such as arithmetic efficiency and flexibility. Therefore, more qualitative approaches are needed in addition to standardized tests of automaticity. This is where the MDA has added benefit, as it focuses on the methods and techniques used by the student and not just whether the answer is correct or not.

According to the new SASC definition, the key principles of an SpLD in mathematics include:

- Difficulties must be unexpected in relation to age, level of education and level of experience which may include level of attainment in other areas of the curriculum.

- Difficulties should be specific and established as persistent.

- Difficulties must not be solely caused by different teaching approaches or gaps in education or social or personal factors which adversely affect attitude/motivation with regard to learning mathematics

- Incomplete mastery of the language of instruction.

In **dyscalculia**, the most commonly observed cognitive impairment is a pronounced and persistent difficulty with numerical magnitude processing and understanding. This presents as age-related difficulties with naming, ordering and comparing physical quantities and numbers, estimating and place value.

Numerical magnitude processing involves the ability to represent and process non-symbolic (e.g. dice patterns) and symbolic (e.g. Arabic numerals) magnitudes. Numerical magnitude processing also includes magnitude estimation, counting and numerical sequencing. The early sections of the MDA focus on these foundational aspects of maths and will provide lots of evidence to enable a focused teaching intervention plan on the specific areas where maths knowledge and understanding starts to break down.

Mathematics is a very varied discipline. Difficulties of learning mathematics may present in specific areas (e.g. basic calculations) or across all areas of mathematics studied by the individual.

Some individuals may not present with a specific cognitive impairment in numerical processing but have an equally debilitating specific learning difficulty (SpLD in mathematics) due to other processing difficulties. For example, difficulties with language, executive function (verbal and visuospatial), working memory and inhibitory control and visuospatial processing may also contribute.

Persistent difficulties in mathematics can have a significant impact on life, learning and work. This may also have a detrimental impact on an individual's resilience to apply mathematic skills effectively. How these difficulties impact the individual learner will depend upon the interactions of multiple genetical and environmental factors. It will persist through life but may change in manifestation and severity at different stages. Therefore, early intervention to support a learner with an SpLD in mathematics will offer the best chance to succeed. The MDA provides the necessary level of detail to be able to support this early intervention.

The interaction of genetic, biological, cognitive and environmental factors contributing to maths difficulties is not yet fully understood, nor is the correlation and overlap of symptoms of other developmental conditions. Co-occurrence with other neurodevelopmental conditions is seen as the norm rather than the exception. SpLD in mathematics frequently co-occurs with one or more of the following: attention deficit hyperactivity disorder (ADHD), dyslexia, developmental language disorder (DLD) and developmental coordination disorder (DCD).

Maths anxiety commonly co-occurs with an SpLD in mathematics, but is not an indicator in itself.

The nature of maths learning

Maths is a particularly abstract subject to learn. What does the number 6 actually represent? Some dyscalculic learners may struggle to recognize that the abstract digit 6 represents the concept that a collection of six will always be six in whatever way the collection is arranged. Indeed, for some people, these symbols may seem like a foreign language.

Maths is a complex topic, involving quantity, language (some of which is unique to maths) and concepts of space.

Sometimes the way maths is taught in schools has an impact on maths learning. The maths syllabus is large and is often taught too fast for some students because of time constraints in the curriculum, not allowing time for revision and repetition, and also too quickly for those with a slower processing speed. In addition, the reliance on rote learning can be detrimental, especially for times tables, where we are testing for levels of memory and not for finding out if a student really understands and can apply their knowledge on a particular topic.

Maths is a very modular building-block topic and relies on firm foundations before one can progress on to more complex areas. For example, it would be very challenging to find missing angles in geometry without strong addition and subtraction skills, and simplifying fractions would be impossible without the ability to calculate division questions. This can be represented symbolically as a 'Jenga' tower, which is made up of lots of wooden bricks. A typical dyscalculic student will have key bricks missing in the foundation levels of the tower making the whole maths tower very unstable. Any intervention we design for the student therefore needs to be focused on these key foundation areas and not at the level being taught higher up the tower or at the topic level that the whole class might be working on. If taught appropriately, this kind of foundational approach will make the student's mathematical learned structures much more secure and will enable them to move on to more advanced topics with a greater understanding.

The MDA tool provides exactly the diagnostic information you need to devise appropriate teaching support at the right level of foundational difficulty, establishing where the student first needs support and building up their understanding and ability in maths.

Other causes of difficulties with maths

Dyscalculia is not always the sole factor affecting a student's maths difficulties. Research tends to indicate that there are many co-occurring conditions that affect our learners of mathematics in addition to dyscalculia. Ann Dowker (2020) suggests that 'Children with reading deficits were four times more likely to have deficits in arithmetic than would be expected by chance alone'.

The British Dyslexia Association suggests that '60% of learners with dyslexia will also have maths learning difficulties'.

Dyslexia may impact upon the following:

- the person's ability to understand and tackle word problems in maths

- left/right orientation which can cause the reversal of the orientation of the digit (e.g. where the student writes a 2 which looks like a 5)

- identifying and retaining patterns and sequences

- memory weaknesses leading to a lack of retention of strategies and techniques, so they may revert to counting in ones

- slow processing – this may be the result of weak working memory, which can make retaining information in one's mind more difficult and will make it difficult to keep up with the speed of tuition.

Development coordination disorder (DCD or dyspraxia) will affect both fine and gross motor skills, leading to poorly presented maths work and hindering copying from the board. This is made harder with visual perception challenges, where the student may struggle to make sense of visually prepared information; copying may include errors, omissions and **problems with** organizing work on the page.

Attention deficit disorder (ADD) and attention deficit hyperactivity disorder (ADHD) may impact the student's ability to focus and concentrate in a lesson, and they may miss key parts of information within a topic area.

Social, economic and cultural factors may impact on a student's maths learning as English may not be the main language of the student, and they may fail to understand some of the key terms that are specific to maths.

The factors that influence maths learning can be simplified into two categories: domain-specific and domain-general factors. These factors are important to developing an overall understanding of the profile of the person being assessed using the MDA. An awareness of this information will assist in developing a more focused teaching intervention programme by utilizing the learner's strengths and avoiding specific challenges of the individual.

Domain-specific factors
These are skills and knowledge directly related to mathematics. For example:

- **Numerical magnitude processing:** the ability to represent and process non-symbolic and symbolic magnitudes. In other words, it is about comprehending, estimating and comparing the size of numbers – for example, recognizing that fifteen is larger than seven, whether written out in numerals or as visual objects. Symbolic refers to understanding and manipulating numbers represented by symbols such as 3, 7 or 15 or written words such as three, seven or fifteen. Non-symbolic numerical magnitude processing involves the intuitive understanding and manipulation without using symbols, often referred to as 'number sense'.

- **Maths vocabulary:** the understanding of maths-specific words.

- **Maths anxiety:** the tension, specific fear or worry related to maths situations.

- **Mathematics in the home:** parents' beliefs and expectations about maths for their children as well as their own attitudes to maths and whether they enjoy mathematical activities, such as board games.

Domain-general factors
These are the cognitive abilities that affect overall learning and thinking abilities and impact across all subjects and not just maths. For example:

- **Executive function:** the ability to get things done, such as the necessary organization skills, time management and preparation for tasks.

- **Working memory:** the ability to retain and manipulate distinct pieces of information over a short time period.

- **Inhibitory control:** the ability to control a dominant response or resist interference.

- **Task shifting:** the ability to switch attention between mental tasks, sets or strategies.

- **Phonological processing:** the use of the sound structure to process written and oral information. This also includes rapid automatized naming, which involves quick access to information in the long-term memory.

- **Language:** the ability to express our thoughts and feelings and how we interact with others. It includes vocabulary, morphology, phonological processing and oral comprehension.

- **Spatial skills:** the ability to mentally manipulate, organize, reason about and make sense of spatial relationships including spatial visualization and rotation.

- **Fluid reasoning:** the capacity to reason and solve novel problems independent of any knowledge from the past.

Maths anxiety

It is worth talking about maths anxiety separately as it can be a huge factor in a student's (or adult's) maths issues. Maths anxiety is the negative emotional response some children and adults encounter when faced with maths, whether it is in the classroom or in the real world as an adult. It is something that can be debilitating for many people when dealing with maths and numbers in everyday life.

Maths anxiety is distinct from dyscalculia, and it affects people of all ages, levels of education and socioeconomic groups. It can also impact those people who are normally good at understanding maths. However, people with dyscalculia who are accustomed to struggle and lack of success in maths often experience high levels of maths anxiety as well, as a consequence.

Maths anxiety is more than just a lack of confidence in tackling a new and more complex problem in maths. For instance:

- It can affect the way a person thinks. ('I have never been any good at maths!', 'I can't do maths!')

- Feelings of tension and stress are heightened before and during exams or where time pressure is exerted on a student for a quick response – for example, in times tables tests.

- At the most basic physical level, students may attempt to avoid being anywhere near any kind of mathematics.

- Physical symptoms may include sweating, nausea or a range of nervous reactions such as biting one's nails or lips.

- Frustration and confusion may lead to crying or a raging temper episode.

- A real sense of helplessness is common and can lead to that student shutting down and disengaging by not listening or trying.

An Ipsos MORI poll, commissioned by the Maths Anxiety Trust in the spring of 2018 found that:

- 36 per cent of younger people (15–24 years) feel anxious about maths.

- 20 per cent of adults in Great Britain have felt anxious when confronted with a mathematical problem.

- 23 per cent of parents of children aged 5–15 report that their child often feels anxious when attempting to solve a maths problem.[1]

The origins of maths anxiety can be from the home, the classroom or from society in general. In the home, parents who suffer from maths anxiety can unintentionally transfer such anxiety to their children. For example, children who are reproached for their errors may develop a fear of taking risks and exploring new possibilities, and may start hating mathematics. Also, parents may unintentionally raise maths anxiety in their children by providing them with an excuse to stop trying when they are frustrated or upset due to difficulties with a mathematical task. A response from parents such as 'Don't worry, I've never understood fractions' or 'Never mind, maths was always tricky for me at school too' plants a seed that may grow into a strong belief for children that they are incapable of learning mathematics. Reassuring your child with maths difficulties is still fine to do; we just have to be careful with providing alternative empathetic ways to support them – for example, 'I found this difficult as well. Let's find a way through this together. It's still really important to learn.'

It is also important to note here that the parents may have maths difficulties themselves and this is what is generating their own anxiety in the first place.

> **Note to parents**
> If you do have maths anxiety or maths difficulties of your own, it is not your fault if your child has maths anxiety too! It's just one of those things. We hope this tool will help you to ease your child's maths anxiety along with your own, by showing you what's going on with your child's maths learning, at the nuts-and-bolts level.

[1] https://mathsanxietytrust.com/official-figures.html

Social factors such as generally accepted but wrong-headed ideas about maths – 'mathematical myths' – may also develop or reinforce maths anxiety for some students. For example, the idea that only some people have a 'maths mind' can undermine positive beliefs around self-efficacy – that you can do maths too! Too often, kids and teens may encounter situations in which it is considered 'cool' to hate mathematics, with people readily stating, with some pride, 'I am no good at maths', as though displaying a badge of honour or promoting membership of an I Hate Maths social media group. As a subject, mathematics is unique, because people are not embarrassed failing in this topic, as they might be in other subjects. In our society, it can be considered all right to be bad at maths. It should be noted that this could also be a way of coping with feelings of shame and 'failure' or low self-esteem if a student is bad at maths – to say it's OK to 'hate' maths and be bad at it because most people are, which may help ease feelings of inadequacy. Our manual and test kit are designed to tackle those negative feelings of shame or low self-esteem at the root cause, so your student doesn't feel them any more and can instead feel proud of their maths ability and confident about maths.

The classroom is also a place where maths anxiety can be seen to develop and flourish. If a teacher themselves is anxious about teaching maths, then they may transfer this to their students. This may be characterized by the teacher's over-reliance on more traditional and formal ways of teaching: use of worksheets, repeated drills for rote learning, assigning the same work for the whole class, teaching strictly to the textbook, insisting on only one way to solve a problem and whole-class instruction.

Most people have some kind of negative maths experience – for example, embarrassment or humiliation from failure, insensitive teachers or negative attitudes from family or peers and traditional rote learning rather than a full understanding of the processes. Maths will then trigger negative memories and thoughts so that these people will avoid maths or subjects or modules which they imagine contain maths. Their preparation time will be much less, perhaps avoiding studying until the last minute. Poor preparation leads to poor performance, which is another negative maths experience, making the student more anxious as underachievement reinforces their view that they are bad at maths.

We can break this 'Maths Anxiety Cycle of Failure' and prevent any disengagement with maths in the classroom and at home in the following ways.

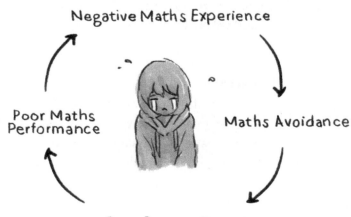

In the classroom

- Be on the lookout for students exhibiting maths anxiety – the earlier the intervention the better.

- Adjust your teaching approach to reduce the possibility of generating high levels of maths anxiety.

- Be aware of the impact that learning new content has on working memory and avoid any cognitive overload.

- Break teaching down into small steps, which will enable the student to have time to process the information.

- Provide lots of revision and practice in class.

- Use concrete materials, such as base ten blocks (even in secondary schools) to help students gain a better understanding of concepts before moving to more abstract topics.

- Make maths fun. Maths games (see below) are an excellent way to reduce maths anxiety and reinforce topics so that students gain a greater and more fluent understanding of maths.

In the home

- Ensure that short and regular practice is included in a plan. Fifteen minutes a day is much more effective than several hours on a Sunday evening – which is something that frequently occurs for many!

- Practise topics that the student has already been taught, including revision and overlearning (see box below).

- Demonstrate that maths is all around in life and should be part of everyday experiences. For example, when cooking, engaging in DIY activities and shopping, encourage the use of maths and make it more relevant.

- Don't pass on your anxiety if you can help it!

- Make maths fun and interesting for your child. Maths games are an important learning tool, but ensure that the game is appropriate for the learner.

- Be open and confident talking about maths difficulties with the child and help to develop a more positive mindset. ('**I CAN** learn things in maths lessons!')

- Seek out resources online or games that can make maths fun!

> **Overlearning** is the process of continuing to practise or study even after gaining proficiency. This helps to retain and recall key information and techniques. This is especially important if the student has memory challenges.

Maths games

You can find a wide variety of maths games to play with children on the internet. As stated previously, maths games can greatly improve maths anxiety. It is often recommended to play maths games one-on-one with a child (one child with one adult). Some examples of maths games include:

- Adding up to ten or number bonds game
- Addition snap
- Multiplication snap
- Subtracting game
- Triangles

(www.dyscalculia.me/anxiety-math-kids)

Each of these games require a deck of cards to play.

There are more examples of maths games and helpful resources for parents and teachers in the 'Useful Websites' section in Appendix C.

So far, we have looked at the definition of dyscalculia and maths difficulties, highlighting the distinction between these areas and noting a lack of awareness about dyscalculia. The key factors that can affect maths difficulties were discussed, as well as the effects maths anxiety can have on students and how these can be addressed both at home and in the classroom with a variety of interventions. In Chapter 2, we will begin to look at some potential early indicators of dyscalculia or maths difficulties and how to gather and record this information effectively.

CHAPTER 2

Indicators of Maths Difficulties and a Checklist

For most children, the first step in identifying a potential problem with maths is that their rate of progress is slower compared to their peers. This may be something students themselves pick up on, through their observation of others and their perception that they perform poorly in classroom tasks or in tests.

In most cases, educators and parents may compare maths performance with that in other subjects, where the student may be progressing with more ease and understanding. When that contrast in performance is coupled with the persistence of difficulties (they don't go away over time), this often leads to the first suspicions of significant maths learning difficulties.

These events often lead to parents or educators wanting more evidence of specific issues with maths or where maths difficulties are occurring. This is where the use of a checklist comes in. A 'key indicators' checklist will help in the process of gathering information on the student to identify key areas in which they may be struggling that could lead to an indication of maths difficulties or whether further investigation or intervention might be needed. These checklists are generally easy to use and are not time-consuming.

The key indicators of a potential problem include:

- an inability to subitize (see box below) very small quantities without counting them
- poor number sense – struggling to estimate or follow patterns
- immature strategies – e.g. reliance on counting in ones
- slow processing speed
- lack of understanding of place value and basic number system
- reversing digits and errors writing numbers (18 is written as 80 or 23 as 32)
- inability to recognize if an answer is reasonable, and inaccurate estimations
- weak at making connections – for example, 4 + 4 = 8, therefore 14 + 4 = 18
- problems with all aspects of money and time – for example, unable to read the

time on an analogue clock or understanding the relative value of coins, such as a small 20p coin which has more value than a larger 10p coin
- poor memory for facts and procedures
- maths language confusion – for example, misunderstanding that the 'difference between' two numbers is in fact a subtraction term
- difficulties in word problems and multi-step calculations
- counting errors (70, 80, 90, 20) and an inability to count backwards.

> **Subitizing** is the quick recognition and quantifying of small numbers of randomly organized dots.

The above is not an exhaustive list of indicators but does include all the key areas to look out for.

There are a number of free **checklists** available which list indicators of dyscalculia and maths difficulties, available to download from these websites:

- Ann Abor Publishers provide a dyscalculia checklist at:
  www.annarbor.co.uk/images/PDF/DyscalculiaChecklist.pdf
  This is solely a list of possible symptoms of dyscalculia.

- Steve Chinn has a dyscalculia checklist – also provided in his book *More Trouble with Maths*, 3rd edition (2023) – available at:
  www.stevechinn.co.uk/dyscalculia/the-dyscalculia-checklist
  There are no overall scores or grades for this list. Obviously, the more behaviours that are present, the more severe the learning difficulties will be. Each indicator is ranked between 1 and 5 so that you can ascertain which are the more serious concerns.

There is an additional dyscalculia and maths difficulties checklist provided by kind permission of the Dyscalculia Network. The checklist has been designed to be used by both educators and parents. It is a simple and easy-to-use form, which provides a snapshot of all the key indicators of dyscalculia and maths difficulties, and presents the information in a very visual 'traffic light' format. Red indicates that the behaviour is often viewed, orange occasionally and green not at all.

If a person gets mostly green with a few orange/red, it would be advisable to note the areas they are finding more challenging and create an intervention programme to target these areas.

The Dyscalculia Network: A dyscalculia checklist

Administering the checklist
Always record the child/young adult's age, at the time of the checklist being completed, and the relevant date.

Instead of a pure checklist we find colour coding easier for the adult administering the test to interpret afterwards. It does involve having a green, orange and red pen at the ready; we find three highlighters most useful!

For each statement colour in the relevant check box:

   Red – often seen
   Orange – sometimes seen
   Green – not seen

If you have not observed the contents of the statement when working with the child or young adult, please leave that statement blank.

The accurate and adequate completion of the checklist is related to the depth of the adult's knowledge of the child/young person and is of course subjective.

The review is also subjective – there are not a given number of red/orange boxes checked that mean the child or young person has dyscalculia or a maths difficulty, but it does **provide a literal, red flag if a child or young person displays many of these signs of maths difficulties or dyscalculia**.

Name: Date of checklist:
Date of birth: Age:

Checklist	Red – often seen	Orange – sometimes seen	Green – not seen
Has high levels of maths anxiety	◯	◯	◯
Avoids maths activities or uses diversion tactics	◯	◯	◯
Is slow to perform calculations	◯	◯	◯
Finds it difficult to follow verbal instructions	◯	◯	◯
Finds it difficult to move from using concrete resources to abstract sums	◯	◯	◯

cont.

Checklist	Red – often seen	Orange – sometimes seen	Green – not seen
Has difficulty with mental arithmetic	○	○	○
Finds it difficult to organize written work	○	○	○
Misunderstands or doesn't retain maths language	○	○	○
Can't see that 4 counters are 4 without counting them (can't subitize)	○	○	○
Finds it hard to count objects correctly (poor 1:1 correspondence)	○	○	○
Has difficulty when counting backwards	○	○	○
Doesn't notice patterns in counting e.g. patterns for 2s	○	○	○
Misunderstands the count e.g. counts from 1 not 0 or counts 80/90/20	○	○	○
Doesn't group to help count larger numbers of objects	○	○	○
Makes errors when sequencing numbers e.g 2, 4, 6, 8, 10, 11, 13	○	○	○
Has difficulty with recall of number bonds e.g. bonds for 10 and doubles	○	○	○
Counts in 1s as a default strategy e.g. 6 and 4 counts from 6 so 6, 7, 8, 9, 10 or 1, 2, 3, 4, 5, 6, and then continues 7, 8, 9, 10	○	○	○
Finds it hard to estimate – doesn't notice if an answer is incorrect e.g. 6 + 4 counted in 1s gives answer of 9 not 10	○	○	○
Often uses fingers to count as a default strategy	○	○	○
Uses tally or other marks to aid counting (not in groups of 5)	○	○	○
Doesn't recognize commutative properties e.g. 4 + 6 is the same as 6 + 4 or 5 × 4 is the same as 4 × 5	○	○	○
Finds it difficult to understand place value and the role of zeros as place holders	○	○	○
Confuses -ty and teens numbers e.g. 13/30	○	○	○
Reverses digits e.g. 45 writes 54 and doesn't notice the place value error	○	○	○
Finds it hard to learn or retain times tables facts	○	○	○
Doesn't recognize that division is the inverse of multiplication	○	○	○

Forgets more complex procedures even when taught repeatedly e.g. short division	○	○	○
Doesn't link column addition or subtraction to place value and finds it hard to line up columns correctly	○	○	○
Doesn't link place value to multiply or divide by 10, 100 or 1,000	○	○	○
Can't tell the time on an analogue clock	○	○	○
Doesn't have a sense of time – often early or late	○	○	○
Doesn't know coin/note money values	○	○	○
Totals			

The use of a checklist of maths difficulties provides an opportunity for a parent or educator to start gathering information on the student's maths ability. It will provide a snapshot of whether the student is demonstrating indicators of maths difficulties always, sometimes or not at all. It does not give any qualitative information on each item, just whether it is present or not.

In contrast, the MDA takes this information further and will provide detailed evidence and examples of maths questions to back up these initial observations.

It is important to remember that checklists like these are not formal assessment tools, but they do provide a helpful first step in the gathering of information on a student who you believe may have persistent maths difficulties, and this can help you decide if a more formal assessment or screening should be sought. In Chapter 3, we will look at maths screeners and further assessment as a second step on the maths checklist.

CHAPTER 3
Maths Screeners

A maths screener assessment may be the next step after the informal recognition of maths difficulties (either through a checklist or concerns raised through general observation) in a student in the classroom or even an adult in the workplace.

A screener is a quick and relatively low-cost option, which can be used easily with a large number of people to identify who may be struggling with the maths learning. They are generally open tests (see box below), which can be administered by both specialist and non-specialist educators. However, people who are experienced with working with students who have low ability in maths may be more able to get the best use out of them and identify more qualitative information, such as 'how' the calculations have been solved by analysis of the nature of the errors made.

> **Open tests** are assessments that have no restrictions on their use. They can be employed by teachers, teaching assistants, SENCOs or a parent of a child whose abilities need investigating. It should be noted that even though they are open, the test results and analysis are improved with relevant experience in teaching maths. The MDA is an open test, in order to encourage widespread use, because it provides the information needed to focus on the maths topics where the individual is beginning to struggle, within a teaching intervention plan.
>
> **Closed tests** can only be used by the appropriately trained and qualified professional.

Screeners provide a limited amount of information and will attempt to focus on what they believe to be the key issues of the maths difficulties or understanding i.e. which areas within maths the student is struggling.

A screener should flag up a potential problem but will not offer recommendations on addressing the problem. They provide information on the individual and should **not** be used as a diagnosis.

There are a number of examples available in the marketplace:

- **GL Assessment (Dyscalculia Screener)**
  This screener aims to highlight dyscalculic tendencies, from age 6 to 14+ and has been standardized to make the results accurate and reliable. The screener comprises five computer-controlled, item-timed sub-tests. The GL Screener tests the numeracy focus and application of maths skills of an individual or small group, especially those students who show difficulty with numbers and arithmetic calculation. This screener uses standardized scores which ensures accurate benchmarks with students of similar ages.

  It focuses on **subitizing** (quick recognition and quantifying small numbers of dots randomly organized) and **numerical Stroop** (identifying which digit symbol represents the larger value despite the different relative font size between, for example, 3 and 8).

- **Dynamo Maths**
  These online screener assessments can be used for students between the ages of 6 and 12. The standardized assessment is baselined for ages 6, 7, 8 and 9.

- **More Trouble with Maths** by Steve Chinn
  This is a short 15-minute test which allows the individual to answer as many questions as possible across a range of (some advanced) topics and provides a standardized score.

- **IDL Dyscalculia Screener**
  The IDL Dyscalculia Screener offers an accessible online assessment designed to detect potential dyscalculia. The dyscalculia assessment typically takes around 15 minutes and is suitable for screening children up to the age of 11.

The MDA differs from the above screeners as it has been designed to focus on the key foundation areas of maths, where the assessment is carried out on a face-to-face basis. This will provide invaluable evidence and observations on 'how' the individual is actually carrying out the calculations on the assessment rather than solely focusing on the accuracy of the answer.

The MDA does not put any time pressures on the individual being assessed, as this is believed to raise anxiety and have a negative impact on the student's ability to do the test without skewing results.

PART 2

Guide to Using the Maths and Dyscalculia Assessment

> **This part of the book focuses on how to administer and get the most from the MDA.**
>
> It has been set out as a step-by-step guide on how to use the MDA. It describes what you as the assessor need to do to prepare for the assessment, and then walks you through the 19 different sections and areas of maths learning the student will be tested on. It includes examples of the actual script of what to say for each section of the student's test, and also some suggestions of what to note down during the administration of the test. Pointers to possible interventions are also suggested, although these will differ depending on each student's needs.

CHAPTER 4
Getting Started

Getting organized

Remember, the Maths and Dyscalculia Assessment is an open test, which means you as the assessor or administrator of the test may be a maths teacher or a parent who is reasonably confident at doing maths. You don't have to have a formal qualification as an assessor or psychologist to use this test kit.

The MDA assessment is an investigation into what maths the student you are assessing can do – and, importantly, how they reach the answers. This, in turn, will allow you to formulate an appropriate teaching intervention plan.

For a successful assessment, it is key that as you talk with the student, you use simple, straightforward language and short, concise sentences. This will make your instructions clear. You also need to listen to the student's responses carefully, to check they have understood you. We have outlined the suggested script you can use in both the Test A (blue) and Test B (red) as well as in Chapter 5 of this book, 'A Step-by-Step Guide to Administering the Test'.

For example, in the Counting section in the assessor's booklet for Test A, which you will find online, there is blue text which is a script that you can speak out loud as the person assessing. For instance, we might suggest you say, 'Count from 1 to 20 in ones, forwards'. As the assessor, you will note any errors. You will then say, 'Count from 10 to 0 in ones, backwards', again noting any errors.

Listening carefully and observing the student being assessed is an essential part of the investigation.

You do not need to cover the whole assessment in one session. We have designed the tests to be split up into different sections, which may be tackled in multiple sessions, to avoid any fatigue or anxiety in the student.

Some people being assessed may not need to complete the whole assessment. Students with low numeracy skills are likely to have challenges with basic number work, such as estimating, a sense of quantity, ordering numbers, counting or reading and writing numbers.

If a student or adult being assessed is struggling with these questions, it may be beneficial (and reduce their anxiety) to stop the assessment before attempting the questions on fractions, decimals and percentages. This may reduce any anxiety that has become noticeable. If appropriate, take a pause and carry on, perhaps after a drink (or giving the student a chance to move around a bit if they need it, to release any tension) or a friendly chat.

What's in the test?

There are 19 mathematical areas covered by both tests. We will discuss each section in more detail in Chapter 5, but here is a list of what is covered in each section in each of the tests.

- Front cover activity (drawing or doodling)
- **Section A** – Number Sense
    - Subitizing
    - Estimating
    - Counting
    - Grouping
- **Section B** – Counting
    - Ones
    - Tens
    - Fives
    - Twos
- **Section C** – Sequencing
    - What comes after these numbers?
    - What comes before these numbers?
- **Section D** – Writing and Reading Numbers
    - Writing
    - Reading
- **Section E** – Early Calculation
    - Addition
    - Subtraction
- **Section F** – Doubles/Halves
- **Section G** – Components of Numbers
- **Section H** – Number Bonds for 10 and Above
    - Number bonds for ten
    - Number bonds for decade numbers (20, 30, etc.)
    - Number bonds for 100
- **Section I** – Place Value
    - Adding and subtracting one/ten/one hundred/one thousand

- Identifying the tens number
- Identifying the hundreds number
- Partitioning numbers
- Using place value information for calculations
- **Section J** – Addition
  - Tens plus a number
  - Adding across a decade boundary
  - Formal column method
- **Section K** – Subtraction
  - Ten minus a number
  - Subtraction back across a decade boundary
  - Formal column method
- **Section L** – Multiplication
  - Single number written multiplication questions
  - Times tables
  - Formal column method
  - Multiplying by 10 and 100
- **Section M** – Division
  - Written division questions
  - Division with remainders
  - Dividing by 10, 100 and 1,000
- **Section N** – Word Problems
- **Section O** – Fractions
  - Visual representation
  - Fractions on a number line
  - Equivalent fractions
  - Fraction calculations
- **Section P** – Decimals
  - To identify the definition of a decimal
  - Identifying where decimal numbers are located on a number line
  - Ranking decimal numbers in terms of size
  - Calculating using decimal numbers
- **Section Q** – Percentages
- **Section R** – Measurement
  - Definitions
  - Measurements
- **Section S** – Conversions

Which tests/booklets to use

For each test, there is a separate booklet for the individual being assessed and another for the assessor.

Start with the Maths and Dyscalculia Assessment Test A (blue).

TEST A (BLUE)

- Maths and Dyscalculia Test A, Assessor's Booklet – use this booklet to instruct the student and take notes.
- Maths and Dyscalculia Test A, Student's Booklet – give this booklet to the student being assessed to answer in, write notes and draw where relevant.

You will notice in the downloadable folders that there are two different assessment tests. These are two different tests (A which is blue and B which is red). They contain the same levels of maths questions.

We have designed these tests to be complementary.

TEST B (RED)

After six months, you can re-test the student using Test B (red). This will enable you to ascertain the effectiveness of the teaching intervention programme that you have set in place.

- Maths and Dyscalculia Test B, Assessor's Booklet – use this booklet to instruct the student and take notes.
- Maths and Dyscalculia Test B, Student's Booklet – give this booklet to the student being assessed to answer in, write notes and draw where relevant.

Downloading the tests

Both tests A and B are available for download from https://library.jkp.com/redeem, using the code GLPUYJM.

There is no limit to the number of times you can download and use tests A and B once you have purchased this book. If there is a problem with accessing the downloadable materials, then please contact JKP customer service at hello@jkp.com.

Some students may find it helpful if you print these tests on coloured rather than white paper, to avoid glare from the contrast of the text against a bright white background. Pale colours like cream, light grey or pastel colours might work best. You can also ask the student if they have any preferences or colour combinations they would prefer to avoid.

Environment/room preparation

Make sure that the chair and table are at an appropriate height for the person being assessed so that they can sit with their feet on the floor and write comfortably.

The table should be clear of any clutter so that the only items visible are those required for the immediate task. People with specific learning difficulties can easily be distracted by things they see, hear or can touch.

You need to have a selection of stationery (pens, pencil, eraser and ruler) ready for the assessment, so that there is no anxiety for the individual if they do not have the right equipment.

> The materials you will need are:
>
> - ten two-sided counters or nuggets for the subitizing and estimating questions
> - spare paper, in case the sheets on the assessment are insufficient
>
> If the student cannot read the word problem questions, then the assessor should read them out loud to the student.

Place/setting

It is important to find a quiet place with minimal distractions, where a private space can be created for the assessment period. The place should be at a suitable temperature so that you and the student are relaxed and able to focus on the task.

Warm desk lighting is preferable to overhead fluorescent lights as the student may have sensory issues.

First impressions

It is important to engage and communicate well with the person you are assessing, so that they feel ready to begin the process. Your body language, eye contact, tone of voice and ability to listen will affect the establishment of a good working relationship. A warm smile and the ability to give sincere compliments will reap rewards in terms of cooperation and positive interactions.

Timing

There is no set time for the whole assessment, but testing trials have shown that it should take around an hour. The assessment can be divided into separate parts if the person being assessed shows signs of fatigue or an inability to continue. Do move on to a different section if a student is unable to attempt certain topics that they might be finding difficult. If the assessment is abandoned, valuable indicators of the need for intervention may remain undiscovered, so it is good to complete as much as you can, even if you skip some sections and return to them later. The assessment can be continued after a break or on a different occasion.

Recording answers and techniques used

As the assessor, it is important that you record, as accurately as you can, what the student does or says while working through the questions. For example, do they speak out loud to themselves, use their fingers to calculate or count, or record their thinking or their working?

There is a checklist of things to look out for on page two of both tests, A and B.

Important factors to look out for and record

- Time to complete: The following box will be found at the beginning of each section and may be used to record the time taken to complete the section.

- Attitude to learning and attitude to maths: Information about a student's attitude to learning in general and, more specifically, mathematics.

- How the student reasons about numbers.

- The student's ability to talk out loud about what they are doing when solving problems. Do they give impulsive answers?

- Strategies that the student uses, not listed here. For example, 'I know that zero means nothing, so I will leave it out.'

Counting strategies

The types of counting strategies a student may use, which you should note down at different stages of the test, include:

- counting on their fingers

- counting in ones, forwards and backwards (for some calculations)

- using tally marks – for example, |||| |||| ||| = 13

- 'counting all' in ones from the first number in a calculation – for example, for 4 + 3 the student might not count on from 4, but start from 1

- 'step counting' forwards or backwards, in groups – for example, counting in twos, fives or tens.

Other strategies

Students may also use other strategies to calculate such as:

- using number bonds to calculate – for example, number bonds for 10 or doubling digits

- 'bridging', where 10 is used as a stepping stone, by applying number bonds for 10 – for example, 8 + 5 = (8 + 2) + 3 = 10 + 3 = 13

- 'reasoning from known facts' – for example, if 6 + 4 = 10, then 6 + 5 = 11

- applying 'key facts', such as bonds for 10, double facts or the 10 times table – for example, 4 is half of 8 so if 8 × 10 = 80, then 4 × 10 = 40 because 40 is half of 80.

Knowledge

Note down any of the following knowledge the student may have:

- any information that is given by the student from their long-term memory – for example, number names, number bonds or multiplication facts

- more advanced knowledge on each topic – for example, 'place value understanding' and the 'principle of exchange' in column subtraction: 12 ones can be exchanged for 1 ten and 2 ones.

> When you are with a student in the assessment, observe and record what you **see** them do and what you **hear** them say to you or to themselves. Also note if they touch and appear to use any materials that are provided.
>
> This will give you a more detailed profile of their abilities and will provide clues to how the student learns and therefore the best way of teaching them. It will also reveal any misconceptions or reasons why continuous errors are being made.
>
> For example, a child may use their fingers for counting in ones for addition. For an older child, this may be embarrassing to them, so they do this underneath the table. Even though they have achieved the correct answer, this may indicate that the individual has not developed more advanced strategies for addition and relies solely on counting in ones using their fingers. It will also highlight possible anxiety issues that could negatively impact confidence.

Now that we have covered the preparation required before completing the tests with the student, we will move on to a step-by-step guide to administering the test.

CHAPTER 5

A Step-by-Step Guide to Administering the Test

In this chapter, we walk you through how to carry out the test with your student, section by section.

Starting out

Once your student is comfortable in the environment and has settled in, you can hand them the student booklet and instruct them when to open it. Have your assessor booklet open in front of you with a pen or pencil ready as well.

The test is divided into 19 sections, Sections A–S. How to administer each section of the test is explained in detail below, but first here are some general principles to keep in mind for administering the test.

General principles

Stop asking questions after two consecutive incorrect answers

If the student you are assessing gets two consecutive answers incorrect, then you may stop asking questions on a particular section and move on to the next one. The fact that they have got two answers wrong implies that they do not have the foundational knowledge needed in this area.

For example, if a student has answered incorrectly for Section E – Early Calculation – Addition on the first two written questions, by presenting

$6 + 1 = 9$

$39 + 1 = 50$

You can then stop asking questions on this subsection and proceed to the next subsection of this part of the test, Early Calculation – Subtraction, both oral and written questions.

In certain sections, if you are confident that it wouldn't make the student too anxious, it might be helpful to ask them to answer a third question. These sections are clearly marked in the detailed section guidance below.

Ask the student how they answered the questions (or why they felt that they couldn't)

If the student being assessed is becoming anxious while completing a particular topic or section on the assessment, you can move on to the next section. Raising maths anxiety in the individual may not give you a true picture of the individual's ability.

Make sure before you do move forward that you ask the student how they reached their answers, and what it is about this topic that is causing their anxiety if they are able to articulate this. Make a note that you are skipping this section and gently ask the student the reason why. If they can't give you a reason, that's fine; just make a note of that and move on.

Using the detailed section explanations in this chapter

> **Important note**
> This section of the manual will make most sense and be most useful if you read through it with the online test assessor booklet open at the same time. This will mean you can see the full sections on the page and how they work before you begin testing the student. And it will enable you to familiarize yourself with the format and content of the test.

Completing the front cover of the student's booklet

Ensure that all the information is filled in before you start the assessment: name, age, date of birth, date of the assessment and the current school year. The first thing that the assessor asks the student is presented as:

> **Assessor script:** Draw a picture of yourself.

The self-portrait is included here to help reduce any anxiety present when taking a test. It should be viewed as a warm-up exercise without any pressure put on the student. If they would rather doodle instead, that's OK, as long as they do so with attention and it relaxes them.

> **Assessor script:** Now, draw a clock face with all the numbers and hands of the clock included.

There are no scores for these activities.

What to note

Make a note of:

- the student's pencil grip, which, if weak, may affect their ability to record numbers accurately and consistently

- the student's visuospatial skills, when aligning numbers on a round clock face.

For the student, drawing images may reduce any maths anxiety, and it can also give you information about 'how they feel about themselves'. The clock-face drawing will give you a snapshot of issues with left/right confusion and visuospatial skills. It also helps the student relax and have some fun.

Here is an example from a recent assessment where the student was very anxious and demonstrated left/right confusion throughout the tests. He also recorded a number reversal for 12.

SECTION A – NUMBER SENSE

Subitizing

This is the ability to rapidly and accurately recognize the number of objects in a small group without having to orally or physically count them.

Arrange four counters in a random grouping.

> **Assessor script:** How many counters are there?

Note whether they are able to identify straightaway the number of counters or if they had to count them.

Estimating

Dyscalculic learners typically will have difficulty with the task of estimating, and this means that they may not notice if their answer is realistic, even if they do self-check their work.

Arrange 10 randomly spaced counters.

> **Assessor script:** Estimate how many counters there are now. How many counters do you think there are?

Note whether they can estimate the number of counters displayed and if there is an understanding of the term 'estimate'.

Allow them to give an answer.

Counting

> **Assessor script:** Now, please count them.

Note how they count and if they use their fingers and touch each counter.

Grouping

This task will identify fine or gross motor issues in the student being assessed. It will also allow you to identify how and whether they use planning and to note which organization skills they use to produce accurate groups of five.

> **Assessor script:** Put these candles into groups of 5 and see if there are any candles left at the end. Write the remainder in the box.

Note the technique that the student uses here and if they demonstrate good attention to detail and are well organized. It would be helpful to record if the student self-checked the sets of five once the task was completed, as this habit will be useful to them during future learning.

Scoring and recording time

- Tick correct answers in the boxes provided and note the total of correct scores for the section at the end of the page.

- There are four marks available in this section.

- If you are recording the time taken for the assessment, write the time taken for each section in the appropriate box.

SECTION B – COUNTING

This section looks at the ability to count forwards and backwards.

Ones

> **Assessor script:** Count from 1 to 20 in ones, forwards.

Wait for them to finish counting, then continue.

> **Assessor script:** Count from 10 to 0 in ones, backwards.

Tens

> **Assessor script:** Count from 10 to 100 in tens, forwards.

Wait for them to finish counting, then continue.

> **Assessor script:** Count from 100 to 200 in tens, forwards.

Wait for them to finish counting, then continue.

> **Assessor script:** Count from 100 to 0 in tens, backwards.

Fives

> **Assessor script:** Count from 5 to 50, in fives, forwards.

Wait for them to finish counting, then continue.

> **Assessor script:** Count from 50 to 0 in fives, backwards.

Twos

> **Assessor script:** Count from 2 to 20 in twos, forwards.

Wait for them to finish counting, then continue.

> **Assessor script:** Count from 20 to 0 in twos, backwards.

Scoring and recording time

- Tick correct answers in the boxes provided and note the total of correct scores for the section at the end of the page.

- There are nine marks available in this section.

- If you are recording the time taken for the assessment, write the time taken for each section in the appropriate box.

SECTION C – SEQUENCING

In this section, you are looking to see if the student can sequence – that is, identify what number comes 'after' and 'before' any given number. Questions are given orally and in written form.

What comes after these numbers?

> **Assessor script:** We're going to look at what comes **after** certain numbers. Tell me what number comes immediately after 8? You don't need to write this down. Now, complete these written questions in your booklet and write down the number that comes next.

A STEP-BY-STEP GUIDE TO ADMINISTERING THE TEST

Test A (blue)
Oral question: What number comes after 8?
Written questions:

12, 13, ▢

47, 48, 49, ▢ , ▢

180, ▢

439, ▢

599, ▢

Test B (red)
Oral question: What number comes after 8?
Written questions:

14, 15, ▢

57, 58, 59, ▢ , ▢

190, ▢

569, ▢

699, ▢

What comes before these numbers?

Assessor script: We're going to look at what comes **before** certain numbers. Tell me what comes immediately before 7? Now, complete these written questions.

The questions from the booklet in Test A and Test B are below.

Test A (blue)
Oral question: What number comes before 7?
Written questions:

▢ , ▢ , 21

▢ , 280

▢ , 300

Test B (red)
Oral question: What number comes before 7?
Written questions:

▢ , ▢ , 31

▢ , 290

▢ , 400

Scoring and recording time

- Tick correct answers in the boxes provided and note the total of correct scores for the section at the end of the page.

- There are 12 marks available in this section.

- If you are recording the time taken for the assessment, write the time taken for each section in the appropriate box.

49

SECTION D – WRITING AND READING NUMBERS

This section looks at the writing and reading of numbers. It enables you to assess the student's ability to read and record numbers from single digits into the thousands.

Writing

Assessor script (wait for the student to complete each task before moving on to the next question). Next, write these numbers.

From 1 to 10
From 11 to 20

Can you write these numbers?

Test A (blue)	Test B (red)
27, 72, 90, 101, 110, 140, 1,005, 6,240	38, 83, 90, 103, 110, 160, 1,008, 5,360

Scoring and recording time

- Tick correct answers in the boxes provided and note the total of correct scores for the section at the end of the page.

- There are ten marks available in this section.

- If you are recording the time taken for the assessment, write the time taken for each section in the appropriate box.

Reading

Here you are looking at how well the student can read numbers. As with all the sections, it is graded by difficulty.

Assessor script: Now, please read out these numbers (indicate or point to the numbers in their student booklet).

Test A (blue)	**Test B (red)**
4, 11, 13, 30, 104, 207, 817, 1,009	5, 12, 15, 50, 106, 308, 918, 1,006

If the student has successfully read out the numbers above, you may ask them to read the larger numbers in their booklets (below).

Test A (blue)	**Test B (red)**
76,125 1,305,703	86,251 2,407,804

Scoring and recording time

- Tick correct answers in the boxes provided and note the total of correct scores for the section at the end of the page.

- There are ten marks available in this section.

- If you are recording the time taken for the assessment, write the time taken for each section in the appropriate box.

SECTION E – EARLY CALCULATION

When we look at early calculation, we ask the questions out loud and also in written form. We include adding and subtracting one or two on to a given number.

This early calculation section looks at the individual's ability to answer these questions relatively quickly, in less than five seconds.

Addition

> **Assessor script:** I am going to ask you some questions now. You don't need to write down the answer, just say the answer back to me.
>
> What is one more than five?
> What is seven plus one?

What is fourteen add one?

What is sixty-nine plus two?

Now, please complete these written questions (indicate the written questions in the student booklet).

Test A (blue)

6 + 1 =
39 + 1 =
7 + 2 =
29 + 2 =

Test B (red)

5 + 1 =
49 + 1 =
6 + 2 =
39 + 2 =

Subtraction

Assessor script: I am going to ask you some questions now. You don't need to write down the answer, just say the answer back to me.

What is one less than three?
What is six minus one?
What is seventeen take away two?
What is thirty-one subtract two?

Now, please complete these written questions (indicate the written questions in the student booklet).

Test A (blue)

3 − 1 =
16 − 1 =
9 − 2 =
51 − 2 =

Test B (red)

5 − 1 =
14 − 1 =
8 − 2 =
61 − 2 =

Scoring and recording time

- Tick correct answers in the boxes provided and note the total of correct scores for the section at the end of the page.

- There are 16 marks available in this section.

- If you are recording the time taken for the assessment, write the time taken for each section in the appropriate box.

SECTION F – DOUBLES/HALVES

This section looks to see if the student understands what doubling and halving mean and whether they can apply this knowledge to calculation questions. The section includes both oral and written questions.

> **Assessor script:** I am going to ask you some oral questions now. You don't need to write down the answer.
>
> **Test A (blue):** What is double two?
> **Test B (red):** What is double three?
> So, what does 'double' mean?
> **Test A (blue):** What is half of 6?
> **Test B (red):** What is half of 8?
> So, what does 'half' mean?

You can then move on to some more challenging questions.

> **Assessor script:** Can you tell me, what is:
>
> Double five?
> **Test A (blue):** Double twenty?
> **Test B (red):** Double thirty?
> Half of 12?
>
> Now, please complete these written questions (indicate the written questions in the student booklet).

Test A (blue)	Test B (red)
4 + 4 =	3 + 3 =
7 + 7 =	8 + 8 =
If 6 + 6 = 12, then 12 − 6 =	If 7 + 7 = 14, then 14 − 7 =
30 + 30 =	40 + 40 =
16 − 8 =	16 − 8 =
18 − 9 =	18 − 9 =

Scoring and recording time

- Tick correct answers in the boxes provided and note the total of correct scores for the section at the end of the page.

- There are 13 marks available in this section.

- If you are recording the time taken for the assessment, write the time taken for each section in the appropriate box.

SECTION G – COMPONENTS OF NUMBERS

This section looks at the student's ability to understand components of numbers. The test asks the student to record numbers in terms of their values. It includes questions involving both addition and subtraction. The questions are in a written format.

> **Assessor script:** Now, please complete these written questions.

Test A (blue)

1 + 2 = ☐

☐ + 2 = 5

3 + ☐ = 7

6 − 4 = ☐

8 − ☐ = 5

☐ − 2 = 7

Test B (red)

3 + 2 = ☐

☐ + 5 = 7

2 + ☐ = 9

7 − 5 = ☐

9 − ☐ = 6

☐ − 3 = 4

Scoring and recording time

- Tick correct answers in the boxes provided and note the total of correct scores for the section at the end of the page.

- There are six marks available in this section.

- If you are recording the time taken for the assessment, write the time taken for each section in the appropriate box.

SECTION H – NUMBER BONDS FOR 10 AND ABOVE

Does the student know their number bonds for 10 and can they apply this knowledge with calculations? This section also explores whether they can extend this knowledge to decade and hundred numbers. The questions are in a written format.

> Note: The questions are grouped for addition and subtraction into
>
> - Number bonds for 10
> - Number bonds for decade numbers (20, 30, etc.)
> - Number bonds for 100
>
> If the student gets two consecutive questions incorrect, if they are willing and it does not make them feel anxious, it would be useful if a third question was asked for these sections, so that you have more evidence about the student's ability for addition and subtraction questions using bonds.

Assessor script: Now, please complete these written questions.

Test A (blue)

Number bonds for ten

7 + 3 = ☐

8 + ☐ = 10

☐ + 4 = 10

10 − 5 = ☐

10 − ☐ = 3

☐ − 4 = 6

Number bonds for decade numbers (20, 30, etc.)

15 + 5 = ☐

16 + ☐ = 20

☐ + 52 = 60

40 − 8 = ☐

30 − ☐ = 24

☐ − 7 = 83

Number bonds for 100

70 + ☐ = 100

☐ + 63 = 100

100 − ☐ = 80

100 − 54 = ☐

Test B (red)

Number bonds for ten

6 + 4 = ☐

7 + ☐ = 10

☐ + 2 = 10

10 − 6 = ☐

10 − ☐ = 6

☐ − 8 = 2

Number bonds for decade numbers (20, 30, etc.)

16 + 4 = ☐

18 + ☐ = 20

☐ + 62 = 70

60 − 7 = ☐

40 − ☐ = 34

☐ − 5 = 85

Number bonds for 100

60 + ☐ = 100

☐ + 48 = 100

100 − ☐ = 70

100 − 36 = ☐

Scoring and recording time

- Tick correct answers in the boxes provided and note the total of correct scores for the section at the end of the page.

- There are 16 marks available in this section.

- If you are recording the time taken for the assessment, write the time taken for each section in the appropriate box.

SECTION I – PLACE VALUE

This section explores place value. You can use it to investigate knowledge and understanding of the base 10 number system. The questions are in a written format.

> In the 'Adding and subtracting one/ten/one hundred/one thousand' part of this section, the questions are grouped separately for addition and subtraction. If a student got two consecutive answers incorrect in this section, it would be good to ask a third question, so that you have evidence of the student's ability for addition and subtraction questions involving place value.

Adding and subtracting one/ten/one hundred/one thousand

Assessor script: Now, please complete these written questions.

Test A (blue)

Addition	Subtraction
26 + 1 =	35 – 1 =
192 + 10 =	213 – 10 =
367 + 100 =	356 – 100 =
889 + 1,000 =	1,010 – 1,000 =

Test B (red)

Addition	Subtraction
36 + 1 =	34 – 1 =
194 + 10 =	218 – 10 =
543 + 100 =	465 – 100 =
764 + 1,000 =	1,423 – 1,000 =

The next parts in this section are about identifying the tens and the hundred digit within a larger number.

Identifying the tens number

> **Assessor script:** Now, which are the 'tens' numbers?

Test A (blue)

46

138

Test B (red)

67

457

Identifying the hundreds number

> **Assessor script:** Now, which is the 'hundreds' number?

Test A (blue)

8,230

Test B (red)

9,340

Partitioning numbers

This part involves splitting up a three-digit number to reflect the value of the individual numbers within it. This is called partitioning. For example, 222 = 200 + 20 + 2.

> **Assessor script:** If 18 can be split into one ten and eight units, how can the number below be split up to show each number's value?

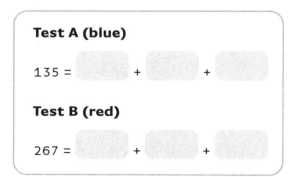

Test A (blue)

135 = ___ + ___ + ___

Test B (red)

267 = ___ + ___ + ___

Using place value information for calculations

The final part of this section is applying place value knowledge in subtraction calculations.

> **Assessor script:** Using what you know about place value, write down the answers to the questions below.

Test A (blue)

54 − 50 =

124 − 100 =

124 − 4 =

124 − 20 =

Test B (red)

67 − 60 =

242 − 200 =

242 − 2 =

242 − 40 =

Scoring and recording time

- Tick correct answers in the boxes provided and note the total of correct scores for the section at the end of the page.

- There are 16 marks available in this section.

- If you are recording the time taken for the assessment, write the time taken for each section in the appropriate box.

SECTION J – ADDITION

This section explores the student's ability to understand the process of addition. It also highlights their preferred method when given a choice. The questions are all in a written format and include word questions.

> In this section, if a student gets two consecutive questions incorrect, it would be helpful to include four questions (two-column addition questions), as they will provide more evidence about the student's ability to understand maths vocabulary, as well as their ability to complete column addition with exchange, which comes next.

Tens plus a number

Assessor script: Now, please complete these written questions.

This part involves adding a single digit to a tens number.

Test A (blue)

10 + 4 =

7 + 50 =

Test B (red)

20 + 6 =

8 + 40 =

Adding across a decade boundary

For example, 7 + 5 = 10 + 2 = 12.

Assessor script: Now, write down these answers.

Test A (blue)

8 + 5 =

19 + 3 =

78 + 5 =

97 + 4 =

Test B (red)

7 + 4 =

18 + 5 =

46 + 7 =

98 + 6 =

Formal column method

Assessor script: Can you show me how you usually work these out?

Test A (blue)

Add 23 and 45

34 plus 26

Test B (red)

Add 34 and 53

37 plus 43

Assessor script: Now, solve these.

Test A (blue)

```
   42          172          105
 + 36        + 153        + 657
 ____        _____        _____
```

Test B (red)

```
   54          152          206
 + 43        + 176        + 647
 ____        _____        _____
```

Scoring and recording time

- Tick correct answers in the boxes provided and note the total of correct scores for the section at the end of the page.

- There are 11 marks available in this section.

- If you are recording the time taken for the assessment, write the time taken for each section in the appropriate box.

SECTION K – SUBTRACTION

This section explores the student's ability in and understanding of subtraction. It also highlights their preferred method when given a choice of methods. The questions are all in a written format and include word questions.

> In this section, if a student gets two consecutive questions incorrect, it would be helpful to include four questions (two-column subtraction questions), which will provide more evidence about the student's ability to understand maths vocabulary, as well as their ability to complete column subtraction with exchange, which comes next.

Ten minus a number

Assessor script: Now, please complete these written questions.

This section involves subtracting a single digit from a tens number.

Test A (blue)

10 − 7 =

40 − 4 =

Test B (red)

10 − 6 =

50 − 3 =

Subtraction back across a decade boundary

For example, 11 − 5 = 6.

| **Assessor script:** Next, write down these answers.

Test A (blue)

12 − 5 =

23 − 4 =

91 − 2 =

102 − 3 =

Test B (red)

13 − 7 =

34 − 6 =

81 − 2 =

103 − 5 =

Formal column method

| **Assessor script:** Can you show me how you usually work these questions out?

Test A (blue)

Subtract 23 from 54:

Find the difference between 82 and 47:

Test B (red)

Subtract 52 from 67:

Find the difference between 94 and 68:

Assessor script: Now, solve these:

Test A (blue)

```
   27          64         810
 - 13        - 18       - 178
 ____        ____       _____
```

Test B (red)

```
   37          74         830
 - 14        - 26       - 172
 ____        ____       _____
```

Scoring and recording time

- Tick correct answers in the boxes provided and note the total of correct scores for the section at the end of the page.

- There are 11 marks available in this section.

- If you are recording the time taken for the assessment, write the time taken for each section in the appropriate box.

SECTION L – MULTIPLICATION

This section explores the student's ability in and understanding of multiplication, including questions for multiplying a given number by ten or by one hundred.

The questions are all in a written format and include a 'smiley' chart to allow the student to indicate how confident they feel about each times table. There is also an option for them to decide their preferred method for formal column multiplication.

Assessor script: Can you tell me what the maths sign ✗ means?

There is a line for the student to write down their answer.

Single number written multiplication questions

Assessor script: Now, complete these written questions.

Test A (blue)

3 × 2 = 　　　　　5 × 3 =

9 × 4 = 　　　　　7 × 6 =

Test B (red)

2 × 3 = 　　　　　3 × 5 =

4 × 9 = 　　　　　6 × 7 =

Times tables

Assessor script: Write down the times tables you are confident about, the ones you are working on and the ones you don't feel confident about in the relevant smiley face box below.

Test A (blue) and Test B (red)

2× 3× 4× 5× 6× 7× 8× 9× 10×

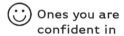
Ones you are confident in

Ones you are working on

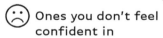
Ones you don't feel confident in

Assessor script: Can you show me how you would usually work these questions out? The grid provides an aid to use if this method is preferred.

Test A (blue)

24 × 3 =

> **Test B (red)**
>
> 32 × 3 =

Formal column method

> Assessor script: Now, complete these written questions.

> **Test A (blue)**
>
>   21   15   23
> × 3   × 8   × 15

> **Test B (red)**
>
>   12   25   34
> × 3   × 7   × 15

Multiplying by 10 and 100

> Assessor script: Now, complete these written questions.

> **Test A (blue)**
>
> 12 × 10 = 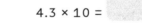   27 × 100 =   4.3 × 10 =

> **Test B (red)**
>
> 13 × 10 =   38 × 100 =   2.6 × 10 =

Scoring and recording time

- Tick correct answers in the boxes provided and note the total of correct scores for the section at the end of the page.

- There are 12 marks available in this section.

- If you are recording the time taken for the assessment, write the time taken for each section in the appropriate box.

SECTION M – DIVISION

This section explores the student's ability in and understanding of division, including questions for dividing a given number by ten or by one hundred. The questions are all in a written format.

There are also questions involving remainders. These are open questions and will allow the student to decide upon their preferred method of calculation here. It will also demonstrate if the student understands the concept of 'remainder' and if they can convert that remainder into a decimal or a fraction.

Assessor script: Can you tell me what the maths sign ÷ means?

There is a line for the student to write down their answer.

Written division questions

Assessor script: Now, please complete these written questions.

Test A (blue)	Test B (red)
8 ÷ 2 =	6 ÷ 3 =
12 ÷ 3 =	12 ÷ 4 =
30 ÷ 6 =	40 ÷ 5 =
45 ÷ 5 =	54 ÷ 6 =
72 ÷ 8 =	63 ÷ 9 =

Division with remainders

| **Assessor script:** Now, complete these written questions.

Test A (blue)

13 ÷ 4 =

58 ÷ 5 =

1,035 ÷ 6 =

Test B (red)

16 ÷ 3 =

68 ÷ 5 =

2,035 ÷ 8 =

Dividing by 10, 100 and 1,000

| **Assessor script:** Now, complete these written questions.

Test A (blue)

140 ÷ 10 =

4,500 ÷ 100 =

3,162 ÷ 1,000 =

Test B (red)

180 ÷ 10 =

5,400 ÷ 100 =

4,535 ÷ 1,000 =

Scoring and recording time

- Tick correct answers in the boxes provided and note the total of correct scores for the section at the end of the page.

- There are 12 marks available in this section.

- If you are recording the time taken for the assessment, write the time taken for each section in the appropriate box.

SECTION N – WORD PROBLEMS

This section contains four straightforward word problems, one for each of the four main operations: addition, subtraction, multiplication and division. The questions are all in a written format.

If the student is not able to read the word problems, then the assessor should read out each question in turn. This is not a test of the student's reading ability; it is used to investigate their maths comprehension where the question is word based. You should be able to identify whether they are able to determine from the words in the question which operation each question requires, and to solve that maths equation.

> It would be helpful to include all four questions in this section with the student, despite making errors in the first two questions, as they will provide evidence on all four operations expressed as word problems.

Assessor script: Now, read and answer these questions.

Test A (blue)

Sam had 6 sweets. His mum gave him 3 more. How many sweets did Sam have then?

There were 7 ducks on a pond. 3 ducks flew away. How many ducks were still on the pond?

There were 4 ponds. There were 2 swans on each pond. How many swans were there altogether?

12 girls were told to get into teams with 3 people in each. How many teams were there?

Test B (red)

Sam had 5 sweets. His mum gave him 4 more. How many sweets did Sam have then?

There were 8 ducks on a pond. 5 ducks flew away. How many ducks were still on the pond?

> There were 6 ponds. There were 3 swans on each pond. How many swans were there altogether?
>
> 16 girls were told to get into teams with 4 people in each. How many teams were there?

Scoring and recording time

- Tick correct answers in the boxes provided and note the total of correct scores for the section at the end of the page.

- There are four marks available in this section.

- If you are recording the time taken for the assessment, write the time taken for each section in the appropriate box.

SECTION O – FRACTIONS

The questions on fractions cover all the different aspects of this topic, ranging from visual representation, fractions represented on a number line, equivalent fractions and calculations using all four operations. The questions are all in a written format.

Visual representation

> **Assessor script:** The fraction of the first circle is written next to it as an example. What fraction of the second circle is shaded?

Test A (blue) and Test B (red)

> **Assessor script:** Which shape has exactly half shaded?

Test A (blue) and Test B (red)

Fractions on a number line

| **Assessor script:** Write the missing fraction on the number line.

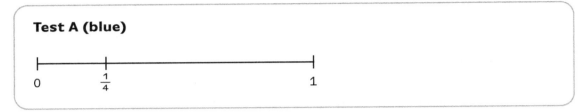

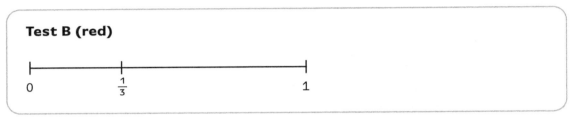

| **Assessor script:** Draw an arrow to show where ¾ is on the number line.

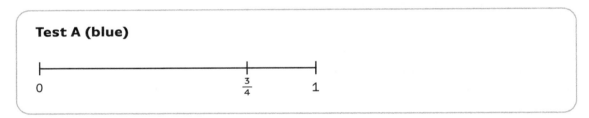

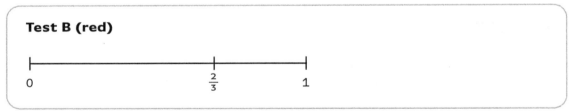

Equivalent fractions

| **Assessor script:** Write the missing number of this equation.

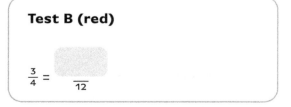

| **Assessor script:** Now, circle the fractions which are equivalent to or have the same value as three-quarters (two-thirds if doing test B).

A STEP-BY-STEP GUIDE TO ADMINISTERING THE TEST

Test A (blue)

(③/④)   6/8   1/2   9/12   2/3   13/14

Test B (red)

(②/③)   4/6   6/12   8/12   1/4   12/13

Fraction calculations

| **Assessor script:** Now, complete these written questions.

Test A (blue)

$\frac{3}{8} + \frac{1}{8} =$ ☐

$1 - \frac{1}{3} =$ ☐

What is $\frac{1}{4}$ of 16? ☐

$\frac{1}{3} + \frac{1}{2} =$ ☐

$\frac{1}{2} \div \frac{1}{8} =$ ☐

What is $\frac{2}{3}$ of 12? ☐

Test B (red)

$\frac{3}{6} + \frac{1}{6} =$ ☐

$1 - \frac{1}{5} =$ ☐

What is $\frac{1}{3}$ of 12? ☐

$\frac{1}{4} + \frac{1}{3} =$ ☐

$\frac{1}{2} \div \frac{1}{4} =$ ☐

What is $\frac{2}{5}$ of 15? ☐

Scoring and recording time

- Tick correct answers in the boxes provided and note the total of correct scores for the section at the end of the page.

- There are 13 marks available in this section.

- If you are recording the time taken for the assessment, write the time taken for each section in the appropriate box.

SECTION P – DECIMALS

This section explores the student's understanding and use of decimal numbers in calculations, as well as ranking decimal numbers in order of size.

The questions are all displayed in a written format.

To identify the definition of a decimal

Assessor script: What is a decimal number?

There is a line for the student to write down their answer.

Identifying where decimal numbers are located on a number line

Assessor script: What is the number marked **A** on the number line?

Allow the student to answer this question before moving on to the next question below.

Assessor script: Mark where the number 1.2 would be on the number line and label it B.

Test A (blue) and Test B (red)

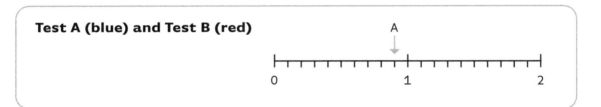

Ranking decimal numbers in terms of size

Assessor script: Next, put these decimal numbers in ascending order (from the smallest to the largest).

Test A (blue)

3.4   3.09   3.13

Test B (red)

5.4   5.09   5.13

Calculating using decimal numbers

Assessor script: Now, please complete these written questions.

Test A (blue)
Add 3.06 to 7.5
Subtract 2.6 from 10
Multiply 3.9 by 5.1
Divide 12.48 by 4

Test B (red)
Add 5.06 to 8.5
Subtract 5.3 from 10
Multiply 2.9 by 4.1
Divide 16.48 by 4

Scoring and recording time

- Tick correct answers in the boxes provided and note the total of correct scores for the section at the end of the page.

- There are eight marks available in this section.

- If you are recording the time taken for the assessment, write the time taken for each section in the appropriate box.

SECTION Q – PERCENTAGES

This section explores the student's ability and understanding of percentages. It also looks to see if the student recognizes the percentage symbol % and if they can accurately describe its meaning.

This section also includes questions involving finding percentages of numbers. All questions are presented in a written format.

Assessor script: Can you tell me what the maths sign % means?

Explain what a percentage is.

Now, please complete these written questions.

Test A (blue)
Find 10% of 50
Find 30% of 80

Test B (red)
Find 10% of 40
Find 40% of 60

Scoring and recording time

- Tick correct answers in the boxes provided and note the total of correct scores for the section at the end of the page.

- There are four marks available in this section.

- If you are recording the time taken for the assessment, write the time taken for each section in the appropriate box.

SECTION R – MEASUREMENT

This section investigates the student's knowledge and understanding of the different units of measurement and how they compare with each other in terms of size and the rate of conversion between them.

It also looks at the student's ability to conduct actual measurements and to draw a straight line of different lengths using a ruler.

Definitions

Assessor script: Can you tell me what these maths words mean?

> **Test A (blue) and Test B (red)**
>
> mm (millimetre)
>
> cm (centimetre)
>
> m (metre)

Measurements

Assessor script: Measure this line using a ruler. (There is a line in the student's booklet to measure.) The line should measure 5cm. Now, draw these measurements with a ruler.

A STEP-BY-STEP GUIDE TO ADMINISTERING THE TEST

Test A (blue) and Test B (red)

50mm long   6cm long

Scoring and recording time

- Tick correct answers in the boxes provided and note the total of correct scores for the section at the end of the page.

- There are six marks available in this section.

- If you are recording the time taken for the assessment, write the time taken for each section in the appropriate box.

SECTION S – CONVERSIONS

This section looks at the individual's ability to convert between fractions, decimals and percentages; mixed numbers and improper fractions; and units of measurements.

Assessor script: Put these figures in order, from smallest to largest.

Test A (blue) and Test B (red)

30% $\frac{3}{5}$ 0.05

Assessor script: Now, solve these.

Test A (blue)

Convert 40% into a fraction
Convert 65% into a decimal
Convert ⅖ into a decimal

Test B (red)

Convert 60% into a fraction
Convert 45% into a decimal
Convert ⅘ into a decimal

Test A (blue)

Convert 1¼ into a mixed number
Convert 2⅕ into an improper fraction

Test B (red)

Convert 1⅗ into a mixed number
Convert 3¼ into an improper fraction

75

> **Assessor script:** Which is the longest measurement?

> **Test A (blue) and Test B (red)**
>
> 1 metre, 90 centimetres or 120 millimetres

Note whether or not they change these measurements into the same unit of measurement before ordering them.

Scoring and recording time

- Tick correct answers in the boxes provided and note the total of correct scores for the section at the end of the page.

- There are seven marks available in this section.

- If you are recording the time taken for the assessment, write the time taken for each section in the appropriate box.

CHAPTER 6
Interpreting the Results

In this chapter, we describe how to use the results of the tests to form a profile for the individual, showing you how their answer can indicate what the underlying issues or areas needing strengthening may be. There will be suggestions of teaching intervention strategies in each section too.

Error analysis: Looking at student errors

Once the student has completed their test, you will need to interpret the results and form a picture of the student's maths learning. In this section of the manual, we will describe and analyse the typical error pattern for each section of the assessment, to support you with your interpretation of the student or students you are working with.

Section A: Number Sense

Number sense is a person's ability to understand, relate and connect numbers. Individuals with strong number sense can generally think fluently and flexibly about numbers, such as 'bridging' (this is decomposing digits to make ten first) to make calculations easier: $8 + 5 = (8 + 2) + 3 = 10 + 3 = 13$.

SUBITIZING

This is the ability to recognize very small quantities of items without the need to count them. Pattern recognition is the ability to recognize patterns on dice up to 6 and from 7 to 10, using two dice.

Subitizing is a skill that can develop from an early age. Young babies may be able to tell the difference between one and two items, or which group of items contains more than the other. It can help children to build images in their mind for small quantities, to be able to visualize and, later, to learn number facts.

This is an innate skill that most young children have when they have developed early counting skills.

Students may be able to recognize and say the correct number word for up to four objects without counting them when they are randomly scattered.

Inability here can indicate very poor skills in pattern recognition.

As part of a teaching plan, play with some counters, allowing the student to view four counters for a few seconds and then cover them up with a piece of card. Ask how many they saw and ask them to check their guess against the actual number. This will help build up their knowledge and feel for recognizing small quantities without counting.

After the student experiences some success here, move on to recognizing dot patterns, like the ones you see on dice, gradually increasing the size of the numbers. Get them to build and record the dot patterns 1–6, verbalizing what they are doing.

ESTIMATING AND COUNTING

A close estimate of the actual number in a group is acceptable. However, a more serious error of judgement, such as estimating 3 instead of 10, suggests a clear lack of number sense and a poor awareness of quantities.

It would be good to check that the student can synchronize touching the counters and reading accurately the number word.

Work on playing estimating games with 5–10 counters, where they can view the counters for a brief few seconds before covering them up. Get them to record their guess, before rearranging the counters into a line so they can actually count them. If they are unable to count accurately, say the number words with them at the student's own pace.

If successful, try for estimates with more counters, up to 20.

If the student is consistently miscounting, they will not be building up a stable sense of number and will need to peel back to more guided practice using activities and games.

As part of the plan, it is important to allow 'visual hooks' to demonstrate how much each number is actually worth. Using dot patterns can provide that help, as lots of students will have some experience of using dice for games and so may have instant recall of the number 5 pattern, for example.

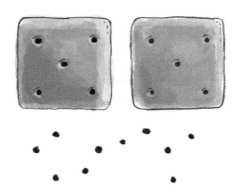

Discuss how much clearer and more recognizable is the dice pattern for 10 (two fives), rather than the random pattern for 10 counters.

GROUPING/ORGANIZATIONAL ABILITY

Included in the assessment is an example that will show how a student may organize a specific task. Here they must put items into groups of 5.

- It is interesting to note that in our tests, every student tackled this differently, so make sure you note how the student completed this task. Perhaps the best way I have seen is when a student wrote numbers on each item up to 5 and then drew a line around those numbers! Mostly, they will pick a point to start and head off in a rush to count 5.

- Note whether they go back and check their numbers are consistent.

- This exercise will reveal any fine motor skills challenges.

- Do they verbally count items as they group?

These abilities can be improved by a series of regular tracking exercises. We like to use tracking on a page containing numbers and symbols, where a student must keep the pencil on the page at all times and circle only a certain number or sign. This will also improve the individual's attention to detail. This is really important because we often see errors in calculation where the student has read the operation sign incorrectly.

Use games and different exercises to organize a collection of items into different numbers of groups. Start with small numbers and increase as they get more accurate.

Section B: Counting
COUNTING FORWARDS

Auditory memory is involved in recalling a sentence that we hear. Auditory sequential memory is when sequences are learned or recalled, such as the alphabet or days of the week, as well as sequences of numbers.

Students with weak auditory and/or auditory sequential memory may have difficulty in counting in the correct order forwards in ones to 10 or more.

The numbers 11 and 12 are unique and need to be learned off by heart, before moving on to the teen numbers, 13 to 19, which follow a more regular pattern. Irregular changes occur to 'thir' in thirteen and 'fif' in fifteen, instead of 'threeteen' and 'fiveteen'.

If a student has confused 20 as 'twenteen', then careful teaching will be required before moving on to the tens (20, 30, 40, etc.) numbers up to 90, to ensure there are no confusions between 'teen' and 'ty' numbers.

If a student confuses the fact that 90 is followed by 100 and says 'ninety, twenty', then correcting this will need explicit teaching, preferably with concrete materials, such as Dienes Base 10 materials.

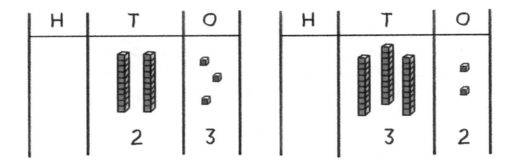

COUNTING BACKWARDS
Many students with memory weaknesses will have difficulty counting backwards from 10 or any number in the counting sequence, due to a probable limitation of their working memory.

Students may be able to count backwards from 10 to 1 as it is fun to count back to the 'blast off' moment, but they often don't learn to count backwards off by heart in the early stages of counting. Therefore, they may have to use their working memory to think as they count and hold in mind what they are trying to do while actually doing it.

COUNTING FORWARDS ORALLY IN ONES (FROM 1 TO 20)
The student should be able to count on, starting from any number. If the student loses their way, they may go back and count again from 1 because they cannot count flexibly.

Problems may include:

- 'Omitting numbers', especially in the teens, and getting stuck at a crossover point – for example, when moving across decade numbers: 28, 29, **30**, 31, 32. A decade number refers to a multiple of 10: 20, 30, 40, etc.

- A dyscalculic student may say '28, 29, 20, 21, 22, 23' or may show other areas of confusion such as 'twenty-nine, twenty-ten', as they may have no idea that the 30s follow the 20s.

- We should also look at the student's counting of the following numbers:
  - **Tens** (from 10 to 100 and from 100 to 200)
    The student may count here, 70, 80, 90, 20. This is an indication of auditory processing confusion between 'teen' (numbers ending in teen such as 18, 19) and 'ty' numbers (30, 40, 50 etc.) where 19 and 90 can be confused.
  - **Fives** (from 5 to 50)
    Difficulties with counting in fives may indicate a difficulty remembering the

sequence of counting in fives (often racing ahead with the rhyme pattern) or may indicate a lack of awareness that five is the halfway point in each decade.
- **Twos** (from 2 to 20)
Hesitation when counting in twos may indicate that the student is counting every alternate number under their breath. They say '2, 4, 6, 8', but are thinking '**2**, 3, **4**, 5, **6**, 7, **8**'.

It is important to spend lots of time teaching basic counting skills using concrete materials, such as Cuisenaire rods, a number track, number bead strings or an abacus.

Use games to untangle and clarify some of the issues mentioned above by talking about them rather than just pointing the confusions out as errors. This may increase the student's anxiety or negatively impact upon their level of self-confidence.

Section C: Sequencing

This section looks at identifying what number comes 'before' and 'after' any given number. Questions are given orally and in written form.

Note the starting point of errors. Students may often have to revert to counting out a number sequence – 1, 2, 3, etc. – to get to see what is next or before but will not be able to use this strategy for the higher numbers.

If students have a poor sense of left and right, this might affect their accuracy in identifying 'before' and 'after' language.

Being able to count from any random number, both forwards and backwards, is important for flexibility.

Sequencing refers to our ability to perceive items in a specific order and to remember that pattern.

In this section, we are considering the student's ability to identify the number immediately before a given number and the number that immediately follows it.

This will provide information about a student's abilities when applying place value understanding and highlight any issues moving forwards or backwards with number patterns.

This part of the assessment starts with small numbers and then looks at numbers into double digits as well as in hundreds. It is common when asked what the number is just before 260, for a dyscalculic student to record that as 250 and the one immediately after as 270.

A number sequence is a list of numbers that are linked by a rule. Dyscalculic students have difficulty identifying them.

The error in this example, may indicate that the student does not have a base understanding of place value for numbers in the hundreds and will require teaching intervention to be focused on this topic using concrete materials, such as Dienes blocks with a place value mat.

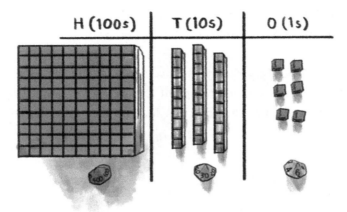

Section D: Writing and Reading Numbers

This section looks at the ability to record (i.e. write down) and read numbers from single digits into the thousands.

Note the exact 'ceiling point' – that is, where errors and omissions begin. You should also note if any digits are incorrectly formed. Does the student start forming numbers from the bottom rather than from the top?

The symbols 0–9 are combined in various ways to form all multi-digit numbers.

WRITING

Writing numbers down is harder than reading numbers, so this should be done first. This is because when asked to write a number, a student must recall what to write, whereas there is a number present when you ask them to read a number. Recognition is easier than recall.

The student should be able to write the dictated numbers reasonably quickly with the digits in the correct sequence and the right orientation.

Numbers above a thousand should be divided in groups of three using a comma or, less usually, a space – for example, 245,927 or 1 359 185.

In the assessment, ask them to write:

INTERPRETING THE RESULTS

- numbers 1 to 10

- numbers 11 to 20

- and a set of random numbers up to thousands.

Problems may include:

- Lack of automaticity may mean that they need to count up from the beginning each time to recall or find what comes next.

> **INTERVENTION:** Teaching must go back and secure efficient counting skills from the beginning of their first error – for example, reversals of an E for a 3, or when 14 is written as 41. Practise number formation using the margin to orientate left/right confusion.

- Digits in the wrong order for a multi-digit number, such as 984, written as 498.

- Writing the second digit first. For example, a student writes 4 then 1 in 14. Even when writing the correct answer, this may indicate that writing teen numbers are difficult or has been difficult in the past and has become a habit.

- Incorrect number of digits. They may write numbers as they hear them spoken, such as 147 written as 10047. This is an indication of a poor understanding of the place value system.

> **INTERVENTION:** Help to build numbers using concrete materials.

- Errors with numbers containing zeros (1004 instead of 104). We can use place value grids to help understand what zero means in a multi-digit number.
  If we read the numbers in chunks, the first number reads as one thousand (no hundreds, no tens) and four. The second number is one hundred (no tens) and four.

Thousands					
H	T	O	H	T	O
		1	0	0	4
			1	0	4

- Writing HTU above the digits as they record them. Students should be allowed to write HTU if they need to, as long as is necessary and useful for them. This is a coping strategy, and the student may rely on it less often, or stop using it altogether, when they gain confidence and understanding.

- Unsure where millions start, and thousands stop. This is caused by a lack of understanding of the place value system for larger numbers. We need to emphasize the repeating nature of HTU for each block of numbers, thousands, millions, billions.

> **INTERVENTION:** Students should work with concrete materials, such as place value Dienes blocks to build visual images. They need to draw their own diagrams to enhance their visualization process and to think using more than one sense.

READING

The student should be able to read numbers accurately and fluently. They should know where to place 'and' in larger numbers, such as one hundred **and** fifty-two.

In the assessment, we have a list of numbers increasing in size.

Problems may include:

- Sequencing difficulties, such as 207 read as 270. This could be caused by insecure sequencing skills (losing track of what number comes next) or by eye-tracking problems, which may require further investigation by a specialist optometrist.

- Left/right confusion, such as 476 read as 674. This is obvious when a student reads the number backwards. You can draw a start sign on the left-hand-side digit to help the student remember this.

- Teen/ty confusion – for example, 670 read as 617. This may be caused by unresolved issues from their auditory sequential memory. Students will need careful training to distinguish the two number 'families' of 'teen' and 'ty' numbers, always exaggerating the difference. Make sure the student verbalizes the differences. They may not perceive or are not aware of the 'n' on the end of the 'teen' numbers.

> **INTERVENTION:** Strong visual image will help here. Get them to draw a picture of a teenager and list all the numbers in that family around the image. Include a sentence such as 'I will be a teenager…when I am thirteen'. Conversely, an image

of a cup of tea with the 'ty' numbers around it, with the sentence 'When I am twenty…I will drink tea'.

Section E: Early Calculation
Questions on the assessment are given both orally and in written form.

This early calculation section looks at the student's ability to answer these questions relatively quickly, in less than five seconds.

Note the following:

- Did they answer the question quickly without hesitation or did they have to resort to counting numbers from the beginning of the sequence – for example, what is 5 add 1? The student responds by counting from the beginning: '1, 2, 3, 4, 5, 6'.

- Did they get stuck on 'decade boundaries', such as 39 + 1?

- Remember to stop asking questions if the student has given two consecutive inaccurate answers within each section and move on to the next section. (See 'Section E' in Chapter 5.)

This section looks at the student's ability to add 1 or 2 to a number or subtract 1 or 2 from any given number – for example, 19 + 1, 21 – 1 or 59 + 2, 101 – 2.

The student should give fluent, rapid answers to adding and subtracting by one and two. They are not expected to know the answer by rote but to reach the answer by their ability to count one or two forwards or backwards.

You should include both oral and written questions because the oral questions give you a good opportunity to test the student's knowledge of the different maths terms. For example, '12 plus 1', '1 more than 5', etc. are suitable, without making the calculation too difficult.

Problems could include:

- An incorrect response 'two more than 14 is 15' may mean that the student is unclear where to start counting. They may think they should begin counting from the original number, then count two to get an answer of 15. This may mean you need to revisit the student's secure basic counting skills and look again at estimating games and activities (examples in the intervention below).

> **INTERVENTION:** Teaching could use a Numicon number track, combined with Cuisenaire rods, where the student creates the initial number and then reads on the scale 'one more' or 'one less'. Once this is secure, then you can move up to 'two more' and 'two less' tasks.
>
>
>
> Playing any type of board game using a dice, such as 'Snakes and Ladders', will encourage the ability to count up, as counting begins from the adjacent number to the place where your counter may reside. You may also play in reverse to demonstrate counting back for 'take away'.

- Note any 'f/th' confusion caused by weak auditory discrimination with sounds 'f' and 'th'. Sometimes students may confuse twenty and twelve as they both start with 'tw' sound.

> **INTERVENTION:** Teaching here should include building numbers with base 10 materials. Ensure that both you as the teacher and the student speak slowly and clearly with exaggeration on the key words, to help the student identify – and sound out – the different letter sounds on the end of the number.

- The student may count all the numbers from the beginning of the counting sequence. For the question 'What is 2 more than 5?' the student responds '1, 2, 3, 4, 5...6, 7'.

> **INTERVENTION:** If the student solves 'plus 1' or 'plus 2' questions by 'counting all' from the beginning, they are not ready to learn to calculate, and you need to revise previous work.
>
> A 'Tins Game' can be used here for visual practice. The first number of items

can be placed in a tin and the number of items in the tin can be written on the closed lid. The student then practises reading the number on the lid, reminding themselves how many there are inside the tin, and then counts on from there after throwing a 1–6 dice, for example. The winner is the one with the highest score counted, by counting on.

- Confusion caused by the terms 'more than' and 'less than'.

INTERVENTION: This will require you to teach the different language concepts using concrete materials, such as counters or Cuisenaire rods. Some students have trouble understanding comparative sizes especially 'more than' or 'less than'. For example, '7 less than 10' or '8 more than 2'.

- Using their fingers. Counting on, for one or two from a number is acceptable; however, beyond this point, they should be using their knowledge of number bonds.
  Students who use their fingers may need to do so for reassurance or out of habit. If they do use their fingers and do so very slowly and carefully, you may need to return to counting, until they are more confident counting backwards or forwards from a given number.

- Inability to count backwards. Many children find counting back much harder than counting forwards, especially when they may have working memory difficulties.

INTERVENTION: For those students who find this extremely difficult despite extra practice, explain about 'finding the difference' between two numbers – for instance, 'counting on/forwards' by using an empty number line.

find the difference
$14 - 8 = \underline{6}$
8 ——————— 14
+1 +1 +1 +1 +1 +1
counting on ⟶

Section F: Doubles/Halves

It is important to know if the student understands what doubling means, so make a note of their explanation.

Generally, when we refer to doubling, we refer to facts about 1 + 1, 2 + 2 up to 10 + 10. If the student is aware of 'doubles facts', then they can use them as foundations for other more advanced maths strategies, such as 'near doubles'.

> **INTERVENTION:** Doubles are generally an easy set of facts to remember as they are all around us – for example, car wheels with 2 + 2 wheels, 5 fingers on each hand makes 10 in total. One of the best ways to teach double facts is to use dice patterns when all of the even numbers are broken down into two equal amounts of a number. For example, 4 is made of 2 and 2, 6 is made of 3 and 3, and when 10 counters are arranged in two lots of dot pattern fives, the pattern of 10 is easy to see.

Near doubles are facts like 5 + 6 or 3 + 4. For the near double 3 + 4, it can be thought of as 3 + 3 and one more, making 7.

> **INTERVENTION:** Get the student to make up their own sums: 5 + 5 = 10, 10 = 5 + 5, 10 − 5 = 5. Can the student explain in logical language that doubling is the inverse operation of halving? For example, if 5 + 5 = 10, then 10 − 5 leaves the other 5.

Check the student's understanding of what halving means. Make notes of the student's explanation but also whether they are aware that halving is the inverse operation of doubling. For example, 'if 6 + 6 = 12, what would 12 − 6 be?'

Section G: Components of Numbers

Components of numbers are the number combinations that can make up a number. For example, a 5 can be made up of a 4 and 1, 3 and 2, 2 and 3 and 1 and 4 – thus, including combinations that display the 'commutative' nature of addition.

An understanding of number components is very important as it allows for flexibility of number calculations. For example, 7 − 3 is 4 because 7 is made up of 4 and 3.

Understanding the components of numbers such as 7 = 5 + 2 or 9 = 10 −1 is as essential in maths as is knowing the role of alphabet sounds in language.

Normally, teaching is focused on the number bonds for 10, but we believe that an understanding of the components of all the single-digit numbers will improve understanding and flexibility with numbers and will boost calculation skills.

The student should have a quick recall of key number bonds: doubles such as 2 = 1 + 1, 4 = 2 + 2 and near doubles 1 + 2 = 3, 2 + 3 = 5, etc. They can then learn to derive all of the other number bonds from these initial key facts.

Problems could include here:

- The student may put up seven fingers and split the whole into two groups and then count each set.

- They may count all the numbers rather than just the missing addend.

- The student may have poor reasoning or a weak memory for these initial facts.

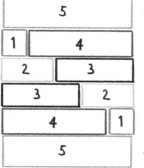

Rod 'Sandwich' for 5

INTERVENTION: Cuisenaire rods are a good way to teach these number bonds as the student can explore the different combinations which are the same length as the larger number. It can be called a 'rod sandwich', with two rods of the largest number being the bread and the pairs of numbers making the filling.

INTERVENTION: The use of dot patterns can also help a student who is having difficulty learning these key facts. By building and talking about them they will learn to visualize the number patterns and will be able to create addition and subtraction equations to reflect these different components.

Section H: Number Bonds for 10 and Above
NUMBER BONDS FOR 10

The number bonds of 10 are the most important number bonds. They underpin calculation throughout the base 10 number system.

A student's recall of the number bonds of 10 should be automatic, or the student should be able to derive them quickly from a fact that is already known. Without this knowledge, students are left with inefficient strategies for calculation. Teaching using concrete materials, such as Cuisenaire rods, bead strings and other base 10 material, will ensure they develop more efficient strategies.

When assessing here, vary the position of the missing number to see if the student has an understanding of the commutative nature of addition. For example, 3 + 4 = 7 and 4 + 3 also makes 7.

NUMBER BONDS FOR DECADE NUMBERS (20, 30, ETC.) AND NUMBER BONDS FOR 100

After checking the student's bonds for 10, we can extend the questions to include bonds for 20 and of 100. Notes and questions to ascertain how they calculated these higher numbers are important. However, if a student has made two consecutive errors in the questions on bonds for 10, do not extend questions for these higher numbers as you do not want to create any additional anxiety, and then it will be clear where to begin teaching for intervention.

The students should be able to apply their number bond knowledge to numbers in the higher decades and also the number bonds for 100. For example, 84 + 6 = 80 + (4 + 6) = 90

Problems may include:

- needing to use a number line which shows they are not able to apply bonds for 10 knowledge

- counting forwards or back in ones or using their fingers which shows a lack of bonds or an inability to apply that knowledge

- difficulty with missing 'addends' – for example, 5 + ? = 10. Five plus 'what' equals 10?

INTERVENTION: We could teach this concept using 'bar modelling', as it is a pictorial representation of the problem, where boxes/bars are used to represent known and unknown amounts. This is also a useful technique when solving word problems and gaining an understanding of equivalent fractions.

| 9 sweets ||
| the rest for Sam | 3 Jane |

? + 3 = 9
9 − 3 = ?

Section I: Place Value

Understanding the concept of place value is essential in order to calculate. It is important, therefore, to check understanding here.

In our assessment, questions include:

- adding and subtracting 1, 10, 100 and 1,000
- identifying the value of each digit
- partitioning larger numbers
- applying place value knowledge in calculations.

Numbers are made up of individual digits combined in a variety of ways. The value of an individual digit depends on its position or place in that number. For example, the value of the 6 in 261 is 60.

The place value grid is ordered into columns. Each column varies by a factor of ten, which gives us our column headings ones, tens, hundreds, thousands, tens of thousands, hundreds of thousands, millions, etc.

Commas or spaces for larger numbers make them easier to read. The commas mark off clusters of three HTO (hundreds, tens and ones), which are repeated inside each larger group.

On the place value chart below, we practise reading the large number in 'chunks', which are separated by the comma or space:

- thirteen million
- five hundred and eighty-six thousand
- and seventy-nine.

Millions			Thousands					
H	T	O	H	T	O	H	T	O
	1	3	5	8	6	0	7	9

INTERVENTION: Students without a strong sense of number will often fail to grasp the place value system and will need to use concrete materials such as a place value mat and Dienes blocks to help secure this concept. For example, if we are looking to understand the difference between 19 and 90, we can create the number using Dienes ten sticks and ones, so that it is easier to differentiate the numbers.

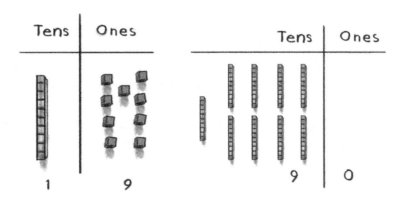

Section J: Addition

This is an opportunity to look at the different strategies used for addition and discover if there are any 'one method fits all' techniques adopted by the student:

- **Ten plus a single digit**
  There should be a prompt response to knowing that ten plus a single digit produces a teen answer – 10 + 4 = 14.

Note the student who solves this slowly and uncertainly, counting on from 10 in an answer, or indeed counting all the way up from 1.

- **Adding across a decade boundary**, such as 8 + 5.
  Note what strategy they employ. Counting up in ones slowly, perhaps using fingers, would indicate difficulties in maths, whereas bridging using the nearest ten or using near doubles would show more developed understanding here.

> **INTERVENTION:** Bridging, for example, for 8 + 5 would employ both knowledge of bonds for 10 and individual component number knowledge. For example, we could add 2 to the 8 to make 10 and then be left with an easier calculation of 10 + the 3 remaining (from the 5) to make 13.
>
> The diagram below illustrates the two steps, with the first getting to the nearest 'ten number' followed by addition of the remaining part of the second number in the calculation.
>
>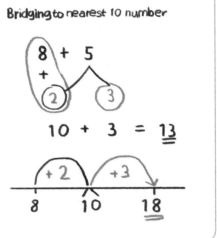

- **Typical strategy used**
  In the assessment, word problem questions are included to uncover whether the student understands the different language for addition. 'Plus', 'and', 'more than', etc. could be used as well. This enables you to discover what the student's preferred strategy is. For example, using column addition exclusively would not be the most effective strategy in all cases and may indicate a rote method rather than understanding.
  These questions also test the student's ability to accurately line up numbers in place value columns, if that is the preferred method.

- **Formal column addition**
  The examples were chosen to determine the effectiveness of the student's use of basic column addition. Note how they add within the columns and whether this is consistent with the other addition questions. Also note if the student notices when they must exchange a number into the next column, when ten or more is the sum in the column being added.

It is important to note the technique used to record if they start from the right-hand column or if they begin from the left-hand column and move to the right. If possible, get the student to verbalize what they are doing and write down what they say to themselves.

INTERVENTION: We need to establish that we start from the smallest-value column and progressively get larger values of subsequent columns. We can use Dienes blocks with a place value mat to visualize the different sizes of each. The smallest-value column will be the one on the right-hand side, and we add up each column moving left, one at a time. It is important to begin with small numbers and only use larger numbers when the student feels comfortable and is successful. Teaching of the 'exchange' principle will take time, and demonstration using Dienes blocks on a place value mat will be effective.

> For example, 35 + 27
> The numbers need to be aligned in their respective columns:
> 35 = 30 (3 tens) + 5 (5 ones)
> 27 = 20 (2 tens) + 7 (7 ones)
> The first column to be calculated would be the ones:
> 5 + 7 = 12 (1 ten and 2 ones)
> The one ten is moved into the next column, the tens
> The calculation in the next column for the tens reads: 3 (tens) + 2 (tens)
>   + 1 (tens)
> So the answer is 62. This is equivalent to 6 (tens) and 2 (ones).

Section K: Subtraction

This is an opportunity to look at the different strategies used for subtraction and to discover if there are any 'one method fits all' techniques adopted by the student.

The assessment looks at the student's ability to:

- **Subtract a single number from a tens number:**
  - Do they count back in ones or do they use their number bond knowledge?
  - Can they extend this knowledge for higher decade numbers?

- **Subtracting across a decade boundary.** This is notoriously difficult when counting back in ones.
  For example, 12 − 5 = ?
  Does the student start counting back from 12 and begin using the 12 itself – 12, 11, 10, 9 – and get to an answer of 8?
  Or do they start counting back from 11 and get a correct answer of 7?

INTERVENTION: Teaching bridging back using the tens number is a good teaching strategy here. Many board games are an effective way of teaching counting back as you need to move back from the square you are already on.

- **Typical strategy used**
  Two-word problem questions here are used to uncover whether students understand the different language used for subtraction – for example, 'less than', 'difference' – and also to determine the student's 'preferred' strategy. Using column subtraction exclusively would not be the most effective strategy in all cases.
  These questions will also test the student's ability to accurately line up numbers in place value columns, if that is the preferred method.

- **Formal column subtraction**
  We use examples to see how effective the student's use of basic column subtraction is, including how they subtract within the columns and also where they have to exchange a number into the next column.
  It is important to note the technique used and to find out if they start from the right column or start from the left column and move to the right. Whenever possible, get the student to verbalize what they are doing so you can record what they say.
  It is also important to see how they cope with an exchange involving multi-digit columns – for example, 8001 – 259.

> **INTERVENTION:** Teaching the principle of exchange requires the student to recognize that 35 – 18 is not the same as 18 – 35, so we emphasize the first number when reading out the question, and it is lined up at the top of each column. We need to use Dienes blocks to demonstrate this process with lots of examples to understand how this works.

Section L: Multiplication

This section is an opportunity to look at the student's understanding and strategies used for multiplication.

The concepts of multiplication and division are particularly hard for a dyscalculic learner not only because they find it hard to learn by rote, but also because they may find it difficult to grasp the concept of working with groups. They may find it hard to visualize and work with repeated groups of equal size; therefore, they may not develop a feel for what multiplication really means and will not retain it over time.

The four times table, for example, works with 'units' of fours. There is uncertainty in the concept of 'four ones' and 'one four', where one number refers to the number in each set while the other number refers to the overall number of groups.

The language of multiplication is often confusing.

For example, '3 multiplied by 2' can mean 3 + 3 but also '3 times 2' means 2 + 2 + 2. For dyscalculic children with weak maths skills, it is often best to use the convention that 2 × 3 means **two threes** and 3 × 2 means **three twos**.

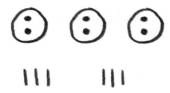

In addition, the word 'times' may not make things clear. Confusion with clocks and time may develop. It may be better to start initially with 'groups of' or 'lots of' instead of using 'times'. For example, 5 × 8 should be read as five groups of eight.

The assessment starts with:

- Asking the student to identify the 'abstract' multiplication sign and what it means. An explanation of what the sign means will give you an insight into the student's understanding of this topic. Often 3 × 2 is added to make 5, as the signs for addition and multiplication, often written quickly, do look like each other. It is important to use concrete materials to demonstrate the different effects of each sign.

- There are four single-digit multiplication questions which are looking at whether the student understands how to calculate simple or more complex answers. It is important to note how they tackle these questions, to find out if they are using a group of dots or tally marks to add up by counting in ones, for example.

- Other problems may be identified where the student may 'step-count' (2, 4, 6, 8, etc.) and often begin at the start of the table's sequence.
  For example, 'what is 4 × 8' may be answered as '8, 16, 24, 32', because they have learned only in a rote sequence, 1 times 8, 2 times 8, 3 times 8, 4 times 8. These complex methods may lead to four separate calculations which will impose extra pressure on the individual to get an answer.

INTERVENTION: Students who fail to memorize times table facts by rote should be taught to use a reasoning strategy, step counting from known facts 10×, 5× and 2×. From these facts, the student can step-count up and down to get to the answer relatively quickly.

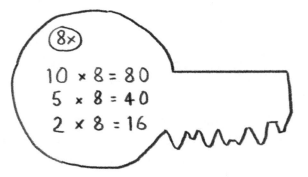

10 ×... is the first key of the 8s times table

5 ×... is the second key and will be 'half' of what 10× is

2 ×... is the third key and it represents 'double' of 8s.

A reasoning approach uses the 'key' milestones as per the diagram above and step-counts to get to the answer required.

For example:

- to find out 6 × 8, I can use 5 × 8 = 40 by adding an 8:
  40 + 8 = 48

- to find out 9 × 8, I can use 10 × 8 = 80 by subtracting an 8:
  80 − 8 = 72

In this assessment a 'smiley face' table is included, which allows the student to rank the times tables in levels of confidence. This enables the assessor to see where they perceive themselves to be struggling and will provide a starting point for intervention on this topic.

The formal column method is also investigated for multiplication, with simple questions extended into multi-digit questions. This will show if they can line up the numbers accurately and if they include placeholders in the appropriate place, and will ensure that all the elements are multiplied correctly.

Examples of errors with formal column multiplication:

- **Multiplying columns left to right instead of right to left** (smallest-value to largest-value column). For example, here the first calculation is 3 × 2, followed by 3 × 5.

- Incorrect placement of the 'exchanged' digit. For example, in the calculation 5 × 3 = 15, the 1 has been recorded instead of the 5, which has been moved into the next column.

- Confusion of what multiplies what within the columns. For example, 4 × 2, followed by 6 × 1.

- **Error of alignment of columns.** For example, the 6 looks as if it is aligned under the 1 rather than the 3, so when the columns are aligned and calculated, an error is made.

- It is necessary to look at the student's understanding and execution of multiplying numbers by 10, 100 and 1,000, to see if they are resorting to use of the formal

```
    25
×   31
———
   615  +
   210
———
   825
```

```
     43
×    25
      5
———
    201  +
     86
———
    287
```
error recording double-digit number

```
     2  1
×    4  6
———
    8  6
```
confusion of order of multiplication

```
    132
×    21
———
    132  +
    264
———
   2736
```
mis-aligned calculation

column method or if they move the numbers along the columns with the decimal point anchored in place. It would be important to note if they use the common misconception of 'adding a zero' when dividing by ten. How will they apply this erroneous strategy to the decimal question?

> **INTERVENTION:** There are many good concrete materials available to teach this concept. For example:
>
> 2.35 × 100
>
> Using the slider (shown in the illustration), the numbers move two columns to the left creating a larger number.
>
> | H | T | U | . | $\frac{1}{10}$ | $\frac{1}{100}$ | $\frac{1}{1000}$ |
> |---|---|---|---|---|---|---|
> | | | 2 | . | 3 | 5 | 0 |
>
> | H | T | U | . | $\frac{1}{10}$ | $\frac{1}{100}$ |
> |---|---|---|---|---|---|
> | 2 | 3 | 5 | . | 0 | |

Section M: Division

Division is the most abstract of the four calculation operations and many students with dyscalculia find it a very difficult concept. These difficulties are not helped by the fact that division can be presented in three different ways, each with a different working method.

$$15 \div 3 \quad \text{or} \quad \frac{15}{3} \quad \text{or} \quad 3\overline{)15}$$

It is now increasingly common for division to be taught alongside multiplication as inverse operations. However, most students with maths weaknesses may not grasp an understanding of division, even if they are competent with the multiplication process, despite the fact that division is also based upon equal-sized groups which are manipulated in both operations. They may say, 'Oh, I haven't done division yet!'

In essence, multiplication involves putting groups together and division involves taking the whole numbers and splitting them into equal-sized groups. For example, if five fours are 20, then 20 split or divided by four makes five groups of four.

Traditional teaching of division often focuses on the 'sharing' model of division, where the size of the group has to be worked out. For example, 'share 15 into three groups'. The 'grouping' model states the number of groups in advance. For example, Group 15 into three structured groups. Most children find it easier to model and visualize the grouping model of division, which can be easily demonstrated as the inverse of multiplication.

> **INTERVENTION:** This similarity between grouping for multiplication and division should mean that the topics would be best taught as near as possible together, rather than as distinct topics.

In this section:

- The assessment begins by asking the student to identify the 'abstract' division sign and what it means. Looking at the question 15 ÷ 3, the student will often see the sign as a subtraction and submit an answer of 12, as the signs look similar.

- The abstract term 'divided by' can be hard to translate into something meaningful, as it can refer to both concepts of division. Therefore, it is important to be consistent with the language used when describing these division questions to avoid confusion for the learner.

- In this assessment, simple division questions are presented, which are extended to include higher numbers. Strategies often observed include using tally marks and circling groups to derive an answer or counting in ones using fingers.

- Division is the only operation that does not give a discrete answer, and it is necessary to investigate how the student deals with the 'remainder'. Do they completely miss it out, write the number remaining as 'R' equals that number, or can they translate that number into a fraction or into a decimal number, if asked?

- It is important to look at the student's understanding and ability to tackle long division and how they tackle the bus stop method of division. Is this their preferred method for all division questions? What method do they use, can they explain what they are doing and how do they approach a division problem when the divisor is larger than 10? For example, 24 divided by 12 (the divisor).

- Finally, we look at the student's understanding and execution of dividing numbers by 10, 100 and 1,000. Are they resorting to the formal column method, or do they move the numbers along the columns, with the decimal point anchored in place? It would be important to note if they use the common misconception of 'removing a zero' when dividing by ten. How will they apply this erroneous strategy to the decimal question?

> **INTERVENTION:** There are lots of good concrete materials available to teach this concept. These operations of multiplying and dividing by 10, 100 and 1,000, are crucial to the accurate conversions between units of measurement.

In this illustrated example, it has been read as 5 divided by 3, rather than the correct arrangement 3 divided by 5...which leads to an inaccurate answer.

$$5 \div 3 = 1$$

Below is an example showing incorrect use of remainder. In this example, the third question should be 38 divided by 5 and not 8 divided by 5 as shown.

Next is an example showing dividing right to left inside the bus stop.

291   r = 3

> **INTERVENTION:**
>
> - It would be helpful to practise technique using a times table that the student is comfortable with, such as 5.
> - Make sure that the student recognizes the 'divisor' which is the number outside the 'bus stop' and the one which we divide by.
> - Divide up each number in the 'bus stop' so that the student can focus on one calculation at a time.
> - Write out each step using colour coding to practise the steps.

Section N: Word Problems

It has been noted by many practising teachers that most students dislike word problems and that those with specific learning difficulties dislike word problems even more than most. These students find it difficult to determine which operation will solve the word problem and often cannot unravel problems that require more than one step.

Students' techniques to solve word problems can be broadly grouped into 'top-down' and 'bottom-up' approaches. The confident and able student who may apply the top-down approach, is able to quickly read the question, identify the problem type, locate the key numbers and work out the required solution.

Less advanced and unconfident mathematical thinkers tend to proceed in a 'bottom-up' manner as they try to make sense of what the word problem is asking them to do. Part of their difficulty is the extremely condensed language often used in word problems. Inevitably, their working memory weaknesses will also contribute to the difficulties of coping with multi-step problems.

Often, their lack of confidence in their own number sense leads them to simply pick out the numbers from the mass of words and guess, by the size of the numbers, what operations might need to be attempted.

Word problems often lead to an increase in a student's level of maths anxiety.

In our assessment, we have included simple examples involving all four operations.

There may be reading and comprehension challenges, so we would recommend that the assessor reads the question to the student. As we state above, this is because this assessment is not a reading test but a comprehension one. The assessor should not assist the student with understanding the question, but should make a note about the student's ability to read the question themselves or any difficulty they have understanding the actual question. This may only be apparent if the student asks the assessor what the question means.

> **INTERVENTION:**
>
> - Start with familiar 'fun' topics, such as netball or football.
> - Ensure small numbers are used initially.
> - Verbalize the problem and encourage them to draw diagrams to reflect it.
> - Use highlighters to identify key terms and parts of the question.
> - Use concrete materials to show relationships.
> - Use simple colloquial language.

As educators and adults, we need to be careful how we phrase questions. Often, the way we phrase word problems makes things more confusing for students and adults with dyscalculia or maths difficulties.

For example: Sam has 3 sweets. Jane also has some sweets. Sam and Jane have 9 sweets altogether. How many sweets does Jane have?

This is much better written as: There are 9 sweets; 3 of them belong to Jane. The rest of the sweets belong to Sam. How many sweets does Sam have?

We can use bar modelling to demonstrate this problem visually.

$$? + 3 = 9$$
$$9 - 3 = ?$$

Section O: Fractions

What is a fraction? It comes from the Latin word fractus, meaning part of a whole, or broken or divided part of a number, similar to the components of a number. Here, a 'whole' refers to a complete object before it is split into fractions. For example, a sheet of A4 paper, a cake, pizza or a shape.

Dyscalculic students, in common with many other students, have particular difficulties with fractions. A large part of the problem is holding on to the concept of fractions – that is, when a whole is split into parts, those parts must still be seen in relation to a whole.

Students learn that when a whole is split into four parts, each part can be described as 'one out of four' parts and given the specific label 'one-quarter' and written as ¼. Dyscalculic students tend to see any segmented whole as something which has been split into smaller 'wholes'. For example, if you cut a cake into four equal slices, they tend to see four cake slices, rather than quarters of one cake.

The basic confusion makes it very difficult for such students to:

- visualize fractional forms

- hold on to the descriptive term for top number (numerator) and bottom number (denominator)

- interpret the sizes of fractional shapes in relation to each other – for example, the fact that ¼ is larger than ⅛. It can be very difficult to comprehend that when the denominator gets larger, the size of the fraction of a whole gets smaller.

> **INTERVENTION:** The best way to demonstrate that ¼ is bigger than ⅛ is to fold a sheet of A4 paper. Fold it into two equal parts to show halves. Then fold it again to get four quarters, and finally fold it once more to get eight eighths. It can clearly be seen that the section of the sheet of paper representing eighths is smaller than the four sections of quarters.

Note that fractions are often typed or printed with a diagonal line, but teachers should show numbers in a fraction divided by a horizontal line, since the line in a fraction is a division line. This could be confusing, but we are trying to find out what the student's confusions and misconceptions are.

Fractions represent a large topic area, and in the assessment, we have tried to include most of the different aspects that contribute to a basic understanding of the subject.

In the assessment we are looking into the student's understanding of:

- Visual pattern identification of fractions.

- Can a student read a fraction from a diagram? We often use circular diagrams (pizzas and cakes) to represent different fractions, but it is sometimes difficult to visualize equivalence and relative size of fractions with circles, and it is better to use clear visual linear representations, especially if we have grids in the exercise books containing large 'centimetre squares'.

- Errors could include the student confusing the meaning of the denominator (the number of equal parts in the whole).

- Adding fractions to a number line. Professor Butterworth suggests that being able to identify fractions on a number line implies a deeper level of understanding of fractions.

- The concept of equivalent fractions. Does a student understand that two fractions may have the same value even if they are written differently? This is key to allowing the student to be able to compare the relative size and to calculate with fractions.

- Calculation of fractions using all four operations.
  – Does the student understand that you cannot add or subtract fractions easily when the denominators are different? Are they able to subtract fractions from whole numbers?
  – Can the student divide fractions? This is a particularly difficult topic to teach and a good way is to use the grouping model for division.
    For example, 'four divided by a half' can be translated as 'how many halves are there in four wholes?' The reasoning solution to this is: 'In every whole

item, there can be two halves created, so for each one of these four separate whole items there are two halves (4 × 2 = 8); therefore, there are eight halves in four'.

- Converting between mixed numbers and improper fractions and vice versa. Does the student understand the definition of improper fractions and mixed numbers? Do they understand that there are three different ways to write a division question, and in fact 13/4 can be written as 13 divided by 4, which is the equivalent of 3¼. Lots of practice on converting between these mixed numbers and improper fractions, and vice versa, is needed before attempting calculations here.

- Fractions of numbers. Does the student realize that the word 'of' translates into a **multiplication** sign? At the same time, are they aware that to find a fraction of a number, the operation they perform is **division**? For example, find half of 12? The question can be written as ½ × 12, which is solved by dividing 12 by 2 or 12/2. How many twos are there in 12? The answer is six.

> **INTERVENTION:** The teaching plan for fractions has to be visual and utilize concrete materials to demonstrate the relationship between them. It is important to proceed slowly, step by step, to ensure each stage is secure before moving forward.
>
> We can use bar models to illustrate how to find three-fifths of ten. Initially, we can find one-fifth by dividing 10 by 5 which makes 2. Then, knowing that one-fifth is 2, three-fifths would be 2 × 3, which equals 6.

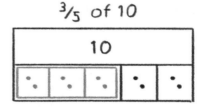

Section P: Decimals

A decimal is a number expressed in the scale of tens. For example, commonly speaking, we talk about decimals when numbers include a decimal point to represent a whole number plus a fraction of a whole number (tenths, hundredths, etc.).

It is important to teach an understanding of decimals using a place value chart to explore the relationship between each column, located to the right of zero, between 0 and 1 to begin with. There is also a need to emphasize the suffix 'th' for these decimal column names – tenths, hundredths – so that the student can differentiate between these numbers which are smaller than one whole and those numbers – tens and hundreds – which are larger than one whole.

Decimal Place Value Chart

In the assessment we are looking into the student's understanding of:

- What is a decimal number? Does the student understand what the decimal point refers to and its meaning? Where would the decimal number be located on a number line?

- Where decimal numbers sit on a number line. Does the student appreciate that decimals divide a whole number into ten parts and these are tenths?

- Arranging decimal numbers in order of size. This will provide us with information on the student's knowledge and understanding of the decimal place value system. Does the student focus primarily on the 'size' of the numeral and think that a numeral with an additional place is for a greater number because the numeral is longer?

- The importance here is to identify where the breakdown occurs, so you can work to remedy it.
    - For example, is 0.15 greater than 0.4 because 15 is larger than 4?
    - Or is 0.9 smaller than 0.25 because 9 is smaller than 25?

- Does the student understand the significance when there is a 'zero' placeholder in a decimal number? For example, which is larger 0.02 or 0.1?

- Calculating using decimal numbers. Does the student line up the decimal numbers using the decimal point when adding, subtracting or dividing decimal numbers? In this example, the numbers are not aligned correctly as the decimal points are not in the same column.

$$13 \cdot 25 + 6 \cdot 5$$

$$\begin{array}{r} 13 \cdot 25 \\ + 6 \cdot 5 \\ \hline 13 \cdot 90 \end{array}$$

What technique does the student use when multiplying decimal numbers and can they estimate to see if their answer is realistic? For example, 2.1 × 3.9. Estimating (2 × 4) would give us an approximate answer of 8.

A student who lines up the decimal point in columns, even though they may accurately multiply each combination of numbers, with the decimal point included, may provide an answer of 81.9. People with dyscalculia struggle with estimating and will not realize that the answer should be near to 8 and not 82.

INTERVENTION: It is important to teach the fact that the decimal point acts as a boundary between whole numbers and parts of whole numbers, and that each column you move to the right away from the decimal point, the value gets smaller.

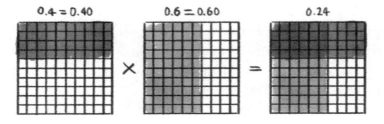

An alternative way of teaching multiplication of decimal numbers includes the use of 100 grids. For example, 0.4 × 0.6, shading in each number with the answer shown by the area overlapped 0.24.

This area model requires pre-teaching of the decimal place value chart to detail what tenths and hundredths represent.

Section Q: Percentages

It is important that students are taught throughout that fractions, decimals and percentages are different ways of expressing proportions and to be aware that we can change between each of these expressions without affecting the overall value. When this link is not established, students see percentages as something different rather than a different way of expressing a proportion. A proportion is a part, a share or a number considered in comparative relation to a whole. For example, a milkshake is made from milk and flavouring. The proportion of milk compared to the flavouring is larger.

Some students are confused with percentages and view them as discrete numbers in their own right and not as a proportion. For example, they may view 20% as the same as 20.

In the assessment, we are looking into the student's understanding of:

- What is a percentage and do they recognize the sign? Does the student understand that a percentage is a proportion of a whole number, expressed as a value out of 100?

- Can they find a percentage of a number?

- Does the student use 10% as a starting point to solving more complex questions? For example, find 30% of 50. The student may find 10% of 50 first:
  - Dividing 50 by 10 gives an answer of 5.
  - To find 30%, the next step might be multiplying the 5 by 3.
  - So that 30% of 50 is 15.

  This is often the preferred method of calculating percentages of numbers as the numbers and calculation are less complex.

  We need to record the technique used by the student here, as some more advanced students may use multiplying fractions to obtain a solution.

  For example, finding 30% of 50 can be expressed as $\frac{30}{100} \times 50$.

> **INTERVENTION:** Once we have identified the technique being employed, we can then help to develop a greater understanding of percentages by visually seeing percentages as 'numbers out of 100' and use simple steps to calculate amounts.
>
> - To find 1% we can divide by 100.
> - To find 10% we can divide by 10.
> - To find 5%, first find 10% and then halve it.
> - To find 25% (a quarter) we can divide the number by 4.
> - To find 50% (half) divide the number by 2.
> - To find 20%, 30%, 40%, 60%, etc., we first find 10% and then multiply by 2, 3, 4, 6, etc.

Section R: Measurement

Measurement is one of the most practical applications of mathematical concepts and skills. It involves the accurate use of the number system, applied to practical situations.

The student with weak maths skills or dyscalculia may have a poor grasp of the order of magnitude of numbers and may therefore find it difficult to judge a realistic estimate of the measurement results that might be obtained.

Students may have difficulties in understanding how to use measuring equipment and get confused with the different units or scales of measurement.

The questions in this section provide us with an opportunity to look at the student's understanding of different units of measurement and to compare relative size.

In the assessment, we are looking into the student's understanding of:

- The meaning of abbreviated measurement terms. Does the student understand what is the actual meaning of the abbreviations for millimetres (mm), centimetres (cm) or metres (m)?

- Using a ruler to measure a printed line. Can the student accurately measure the line? Which unit of measurement will they use to record the length?

- Using a ruler to draw a line of a given length. Can the student accurately read off and draw the length given in the question? This will also test the student's ability to draw an accurate straight line.

- Comparing different units of measurement to determine the longest. Does the student understand the relative difference between units of measurement and are they able to convert between these units of length? Does the student know how many centimetres are equivalent to 1 metre? Or how many millimetres are equivalent to 1 centimetre?
  This will also test the student's ability to multiply and divide by 10, 100 and 1,000, which is used to convert units of measurement.

> **INTERVENTION:** Students with or without dyscalculia will benefit from lots of practical work using rulers of different sizes to actually measure objects around the home or the classroom.
>
> Students with dyscalculia will need lots of overlearning using measuring equipment to help them to visualize the relative size of different units of measurement. They also tend to find estimating challenging, so they may not even realize when they have given an unrealistic answer. Therefore, it is important to keep activities fun and to ensure that the students appreciate the fact that it is OK to make mistakes.

As part of a general discussion with the student, they could be asked about other types of measurement such as weight, time or liquid and what units of measurement we employ for those things.

Section S: Conversions

In mathematics, there are many occasions when you are required to convert between different terms in order to find a solution. In this assessment, these conversions have been grouped together.

- Ranking fractions, decimal numbers and percentages in order of size. Does the student understand the strategy to convert all three of these numbers? What is their preferred format? Do they change these numbers into fractions, for example?

- Converting between fractions, decimals and percentages. It is important to emphasize in teaching that the relative sizes of a given fraction, decimal and percentage are equivalent and should be interchangeable.
  For example, 10% is the same as 1/10 (one tenth) is the same as 0.1
  Can a student convert between them and if so, what technique do they use?

- Converting between improper fractions and mixed numbers. Does the student understand the meaning of these two terms?

- Converting between units of measurement. Does the student know which is smaller or larger?

> **INTERVENTION:** This should include lots of concrete materials to demonstrate the relative difference between these numbers. A fraction tower is a good visual way of demonstrating the relative size and equivalence of fractions, decimals and percentages. Measuring exercises of a variety of different objects using a centimetre and/or a metre ruler will demonstrate relative size and is also a good practical exercise.

CHAPTER 7

Developing a Teaching Intervention Plan

One of the main aims of the MDA is to help formulate a focused teaching intervention plan at the right level of need for the individual. The MDA will provide the detail of where maths learning and understanding begins to break down and so you can target teaching to begin at or just before those topics.

Indeed, it may be beneficial to start teaching in the very first lesson a topic that the individual understands and can do, as this may impact positively on their confidence and help to nurture a 'can do' attitude. They may also recognize that these new multisensory approaches to lessons are different and will help them.

Upon completion of the MDA, the assessor will possess a lot of raw data and information available on the individual. This chapter will provide a guide to summarize this information and develop the teaching intervention plan.

The assessment is a process of gathering data to develop a profile of the individual which details their strengths and weaknesses. This profile should also include background information and observations about the student's overall attitude and experience in learning maths. This information will be drawn directly from the MDA test, but also from the background information provided from the Family Questionnaire (Appendix B) and any additional feedback from educators.

The MDA test can be used to create a summary of what the student has learned and retained so far (summative), and this will be supplemented with additional information regarding what will benefit future learning (formative).

- The Assessment Report (Form A or B)

- The Family Questionnaire (Appendix B)

- A Summary Report and teaching intervention topics document. In your report, you should note:
    - scores on individual topics
    - summary of strengths and challenges with examples
    - where to begin teaching intervention plan
    - date for reassessment.

THE MATHS AND DYSCALCULIA ASSESSMENT

M&DA

Summary Report and Teaching Plan

Name:

Date of assessment:

A. Number Sense	/4	**K.** Subtraction	/11
B. Counting	/9	**L.** Multiplication	/12
C. Sequencing	/12	**M.** Division	/12
D. Writing and Reading Numbers	/20	**N.** Word Problems	/4
E. Early Calculation	/16	**O.** Fractions	/13
F. Doubles/Halves	/13	**P.** Decimals	/8
G. Components of Numbers	/6	**Q.** Percentages	/4
H. Number Bonds for 10 and Above	/16	**R.** Measurement	/6
I. Place Value	/16	**S.** Conversions	/7
J. Addition	/11		

Total Score: /200

Additional information

Summary Report and Teaching Plan

Strengths and challenges

Recommendations of teaching topics

Re-test date:

Example of an assessment using the MDA

An example of a completed summary report and teaching intervention plan is given for a ficticious character, John Doe.

The report scores for each section of the MDA are provided below:

Reassessment

It is important that the assessment process and reassessment process are seen as a continuous process and to set a date for the reassessment after a period of six months.

This will allow the effectiveness of the teaching intervention plan to be reviewed and to fine-tune those elements that can be improved upon in the next period of teaching. It will also show any improvements in scores and whether the student is increasing their understanding of these key foundation topics.

We have created a Form B version of the assessment, where there are identical sections to the initial form. All of the questions have been carefully constructed to enable the same level of difficulty.

This chapter has looked briefly at the formulation of a teaching intervention plan resulting from the tests carried out using the MDA and any additional information gathered by the assessor. It contains a list of general points when teaching, which are essential to a learner who is demonstrating indications of dyscalculia and maths difficulties. The highlighted example of a learner profile, John Doe, demonstrates a guide of how to break down the information into a profile of strengths and weaknesses. The assessment process should be viewed as a continuous process, which involves re-testing to allow progress to be ascertained and a new focused teaching plan to be implemented.

DEVELOPING A TEACHING INTERVENTION PLAN

M&DA

Summary Report and Teaching Plan

Name: John Doe **Date of assessment:** 28-4-24

A. Number Sense	2 /4	**K.** Subtraction	2 /11
B. Counting	5 /9	**L.** Multiplication	2 /12
C. Sequencing	6 /12	**M.** Division	1 /12
D. Writing and Reading Numbers	11 /20	**N.** Word Problems	1 /4
E. Early Calculation	12 /16	**O.** Fractions	2 /13
F. Doubles/Halves	12 /13	**P.** Decimals	1 /8
G. Components of Numbers	4 /6	**Q.** Percentages	1 /4
H. Number Bonds for 10 and Above	6 /16	**R.** Measurement	2 /6
I. Place Value	6 /16	**S.** Conversions	0 /7
J. Addition	6 /11		

Total Score: 79 /200

Additional information

- The assessment was carried out over two periods which lasted one hour in total.
- John worked incredibly hard over the two sessions of the assessment and tried his best to answer as many questions as possible.
- He lacks confidence in maths and worked at a slow pace throughout. He displayed considerable maths anxiety at the outset, suggesting: 'I don't really like maths at all.'
- He had an inefficient left-handed pencil grip which often affected the layout of his work. His writing is very small and he was seen to reverse digits 2, 5 and 7. He said that his hand often ached when he was asked to do too many calculations.
- He used his fingers (under the table) for calculations, where he counted up and back in ones. John did not self-check his work.
- John was not very resilient and would often give up when attempting a calculation which he found challenging.
- His reading was slow and hesitant, which impacted his understanding of the word problems. He did not draw or model problems visually.
- He suggested that he can never remember the way to tackle problems for subtraction and division. He finds it hard to remember the times tables, and when pushed for a quick answer, this makes things worse. He is unable to count backwards and often misses numbers in the sequence, especially for larger numbers around one hundred plus. John prefers to write things down and much prefers written questions to oral ones.
- There is an Educational Psychologist report dated 15.10.2023, which does not provide detail into John's maths abilities. There is also a completed school and family questionnaire which is dated 10.9.2023.

M&DA Summary Report and Teaching Plan

THE MATHS AND DYSCALCULIA ASSESSMENT

Strengths and challenges

From the MDA results, additional information and in conjunction with the information supplied on the family questionnaire an overview of the strengths and challenges of John Doe was detailed as follows:

Strengths

- Good understanding of grouping
- Subitizing
- Sequencing and identifying what number is positioned just before and after a given number up to 100
- Counting up in ones, twos, fives and tens (up to 100)
- Read and record numbers up to 1,000
- Doubles and halving (although he does not always recognize them)
- Components of numbers when adding
- Good understanding and application for column addition, which seems to be his go-to strategy
- Understands and can apply 'exchange' for column subtraction
- Multiplication single-digit numbers (times tables)
- Basic fraction understanding using visual prompts
- Recognizes percentage sign
- Able to work hard for short periods of time

Challenges:

- Sequencing numbers above 100
- Counting backwards in tens, fives and twos is a real difficulty
- Counting forwards in tens above 100
- Read and record large numbers above 1,000
- Calculation technique (he reverts to counting in ones, often using his fingers, even when just adding two units)
- Does not recognize that can use components for subtraction – e.g. 2 + 3 + 5, so 5 – 3 is 2
- Subtraction is challenging generally as he preferred to draw 6 dots for 6 – 4 question
- Use bonds 10 in TU numbers 15 + 5...got correct answer but counted in ones
- Could not extend bonds knowledge to hundred. 70 + __ = 100, he drew 30 dots!
- Place value...even for addition questions he used column addition. He is not able to partition a number...325 = 300 + 20 + 5 to show value of each digit
- Formal column addition tends to be overused...78 + 5 for example, was put into columns. Occasionally he 'carries' the wrong digit into next column...5 + 7 for example, he recorded 1 and carried 2 into next column
- Column subtraction, where he confused what was being subtracted. For example, 64 – 18 was recorded as 54 and 0 – 8 was recorded as 8

M&DA Summary Report and Teaching Plan

DEVELOPING A TEACHING INTERVENTION PLAN

- Does not apply bonds for 10 facts for subtraction
- Formal double-digit multiplication
- Multiplying and dividing by 10/100/1,000
- Language of maths…'does subtract mean the same as divide?'
- Division with remainder
- Word problems where language makes it difficult to comprehend what maths is involved
- More advanced fraction concepts including calculation
- Decimal numbers calculation and ranking in order of size
- Percentages
- Found it difficult to use a ruler to draw straight lines
- Measurement conversion

Maths is a modular topic and relies on secure foundations. Using the data provided for John Doe, a recommendation plan for teaching intervention was compiled, which showed the key areas to address initially to help him to develop his maths understanding.

Recommendations of teaching topics

- It is important to peel back and address the important foundation area of maths. John would benefit from working using visual techniques and the use of concrete materials to consolidate the learning
- Maths language focus
- Correct number formation using the right-hand-side margin
- Components of numbers 1 to 9 using dice patterns. The dice patterns will provide a visual hook to retain what numbers are made up of. This can also be used to introduce equations for addition and subtraction
- Rainbow number bonds for 10 (Reasoning) and encourage the application of these facts

Re-test date: From 1 November 2024

Conclusion

The development of the MDA represents a significant advancement in the educational support for individuals with specific maths learning difficulties. This innovative assessment tool is an open test, clearly designed, and can be used to identify the unique challenges faced by learners who struggle with maths. It will provide a comprehensive analysis of their strengths and weaknesses and therefore enable a focused teaching intervention plan for the individual.

If you are a parent and have issues with maths yourself, you can share the results of the test with your child's teacher, to give them a sense of where intervention may be most useful and where the gaps in your child's understanding are.

The MDA is a vital step forward in creating an inclusive educational environment where all students will have the opportunity to succeed in maths.

PART 3
Appendices

Appendix A
Summary Report and Teaching Plan Template and Example

Summary Report and Teaching Plan

Name: _____ **Date of assessment:** _____

A. Number Sense	/4	**K.** Subtraction	/11
B. Counting	/9	**L.** Multiplication	/12
C. Sequencing	/12	**M.** Division	/12
D. Writing and Reading Numbers	/20	**N.** Word Problems	/4
E. Early Calculation	/16	**O.** Fractions	/13
F. Doubles/Halves	/13	**P.** Decimals	/8
G. Components of Numbers	/6	**Q.** Percentages	/4
H. Number Bonds for 10 and Above	/16	**R.** Measurement	/6
I. Place Value	/16	**S.** Conversions	/7
J. Addition	/11		

Total Score: _____ /200

Additional information

Summary Report and Teaching Plan

Strengths and challenges

Recommendations of teaching topics

Re-test date:

Appendix B
Blank Family Questionnaire

Confidential Family Questionnaire

Your name: ....

Address: ....

Telephone: .... Email: ....

Date of completion: ....

Child's full name: ....

Child's date of birth: .... Age: .... years .... months

Home address: ....

....

Name and address of present school: ....

....

Name of present school head teacher: ....

Name of SENCO: ....

May we have permission to contact school? YES / NO

Parent details (relationship)

Name: ....

Email address: ....

Telephone number (Home): ....

Telephone number (Mobile): ....

Telephone number (Work): ....

Occupation: ....

Address (if different from child's home address): ....

....

Parent details (relationship)

Name: ....

Email address: ....

Telephone number (Home): ....

Telephone number (Mobile): ....

Telephone number (Work): ....

Occupation: ....

Address (if different from child's home address): ....

....

Emergency contact

Please provide contact details for an additional further person who can be contacted in case of an emergency. Please note that these details would only be used if neither parent can be contacted.

Name: ....

Telephone: .... Email: ....

How many children do you have in your family?

Please indicate their age, gender and relationship to the child referred for advice.

Name	Gender	Date of Birth	Age	Relationship
....	....	....	....	....
....	....	....	....	....
....	....	....	....	....
....	....	....	....	....
....	....	....	....	....

Names of other schools attended

Name of school	Type of school (nursery, first, etc.)	Age when child attended school
....	....	....
....	....	....
....	....	....
	Number of schools attended:	....

What is child's attitude towards school? ....
....

At what age did child's learning difficulties first come to your attention? ....
....

What subject areas does he/she find difficult at present? ....
....

Previous treatment of child's difficulties

Has your child had help from outside school? ....

Has your child had help from school? ....

Has your child had any other treatment? (e.g. visits to specialists, speech centres, etc.)

....

....

Please give full details of date, name and address of educational psychologist who carried out any assessment.

....

....

May we have a copy report/permission to write for details? YES / NO

Please give details of remedial help if these are known.

....

....

Development

Have your child's eyes been tested?
Is vision within normal limits?

If NO, please give details of problem..
....

Has your child's hearing been tested?
Is it within normal limits?

If NO, please give details of problem ....

....

At what age was your child walking without help? .... months

At what age was your child beginning to say a few words? ....

Have you noticed any difficulties in talking or communicating? ....

Does your child fidget a lot?
Is child's speech clear and distinct?

If NO, please list sounds which cause difficulty ....

....

Is English the only language spoken at home? ....

Have you noticed your child having difficulty in concentrating on school work?

....

Have you noticed your child having difficulty in remembering:

Instructions .... Where he/she has left things? ....

Has your child had any accidents e.g. head injuries, broken bones, suffocation?

If YES, please give details ....

....

....

....

Is your child left- or right-handed? ....

Is this hand preference consistent or does the child change tools, implements, pencil from hand to hand?

....

Emotional adjustment

Has your child shown any of the following:

Bed wetting .... Approx. age ....

Temper tantrums .... Approx. age ....

Behaviour difficulties at home/in school .... Approx. age ....

Nervousness .... Approx. age ....

Timidity .... Approx. age ....

Fears (e.g. dark, etc.) .... Approx. age ....

Jealousy or envy .... Approx. age ....

Nightmares .... Approx. age ....

How well does he/she get on with other children:

In the family: ....

In school: ....

Does your child have any allergies? If YES, please list all allergies and treatment:

....

....

Does your child take any regular medication?

If YES, please name the drug and condition for which it is taken:

....

....

....

Is your child adopted? ....

Pregnancy

Duration of pregnancy: ....

If premature or overdue, by how many weeks? ....

Did you have any illnesses during pregnancy?

If YES, write down their nature and how many weeks pregnant you were at the time:

....

The birth
Was the baby born at: Home / Hospital?

Birth weight: ....lbs .... oz / ....kg

Total length of labour in hours:

Was the baby's delivery normal?

Were there any complications or unusual features about the birth?

....

....

Mother's age at birth of child: ....

Father's age at birth of child: ....

Infancy
In the four weeks immediately following the birth, did the baby have any of the following?

Convulsions or fits ....

High temperatures ....

Other illnesses ....

....

Have other members of the family (including both parents' families) had maths, reading, spelling or language difficulties? If so, please state family member and nature of difficulty:

....

....

....

Child's difficulties and symptoms

Please describe below the areas your child finds difficult and for which you seek help. Include a brief history if possible.

....

....

....

....

....

....

....

....

....

Maths: ....

....

....

Writing/Spelling: ....

....

....

....

(Continue on back of page if necessary)

Signed ....

Please print name: ....

Date ....Relationship to child ....

Appendix C
Useful Websites with Resources for Teachers and Parents

Dyscalculia Network
www.dyscalculianetwork.com

Emerson House Learning
www.emersonhouse.co.uk

Discovering Dyscalculia
www.discoveringdyscalculia.com

Mahesh Sharma's Center for Teaching and Learning Mathematics
www.dyscalculia.org/experts/mahesh-sharma

Dyscalculia Association
www.dyscalculiaassociation.uk

Fix-it Maths
www.fixitmaths.com

British Dyslexia Association – Dyscalculia
www.bdadyslexia.org.uk/dyscalculia

Hampshire Dyslexia
www.hampshiredyslexia.com

National Numeracy
www.nationalnumeracy.org.uk/what-numeracy/what-dyscalculia

Helen Arkell
https://helenarkell.org.uk

The Dyscalculia Toolkit: Supporting Learning Difficulties in Maths
https://study.sagepub.com/corwin/birdtoolkit4e

IDL: Dyslexia and Dyscalculia Software and Screening Tests
https://idlsgroup.com

Dynamo Maths
https://dynamomaths.co.uk

Laura Jackson – Discovering Dyscalculia
https://discoveringdyscalculia.com

McLeod Learning Centre
www.amandamcleod.org

Bridget Mather-Scott – Billy Bees Learning
www.billybeeslearning.co.uk

Dyslexia Action/Real Group Training
https://dyslexiaaction.org.uk
www.realgroup.co.uk

Sarah Wedderburn – Unicorn Maths
www.unicornmaths.com

Unicorn School
www.unicornoxford.co.uk

Bruern Abbey School
www.bruernabbey.org

SEN Books
www.senbooks.co.uk

Rebecca Thompson – Educational Assessments
https://educationaccess.co.uk

Catherine Eadle
https://www.thelittlemathsroom.co.uk

Pete Jarrett – Tutorum Learning and Assessment Limited
pete@tutorum.co.uk

The SpLD Assessments Standards Committee (SASC)
https://www.sasc.org.uk

Steve Chinn – Maths Explained
https://www.mathsexplained.co.uk

Judy Hornigold
https://judyhornigold.co.uk

Bibliography

Research Articles

Astle, D.E., Holmes, J. Kievit, R. and Gathercole, S. (2022) Annual Research Review: The transdiagnostic revolution in neurodevelopmental disorders. *The Journal of Child Psychology and Psychiatry 63*, 4, 397–417.

De Smedt, B. (2022) Individual differences in mathematical cognition: A Bert's eye view. *Current Opinion in Behavioral Sciences 46*, 1–10.

Dowker, A. (2020) Arithmetic in developmental cognitive disabilities. *Research in Developmental Disabilities 107*, 1–9.

Gilmore, C. (2023) Understanding the complexities of mathematical cognition: A multi-level framework. *Quarterly Journal of Experimental Psychology 76*, 9, 1953–1972.

Government Office for Science (2008) *Foresight Mental Capital and Wellbeing Project: Final project report*. The Stationery Office.

Gross, J., Hudson, C. and Price, D. (2009) *Every Child a Chance Trust/KPMG*. Every Child a Chance Trust.

Mishra, A. and Khan, A. (2022) Domain-general and domain-specific cognitive correlates of developmental dyscalculia: A systematic review of the last two decades' literature. *Child Neuropsychology 29*, 8, 1179–1229.

Morsanyi, K., van Bers, B.M.C.W., McCormack, T. and McGourty, J. (2018) The prevalence of specific learning disorder in mathematics and comorbidity with other developmental disorders in primary school age children. *British Journal of Psychology 109*, 4, 917–940.

Vogel, S.E. and De Smedt, B. (2021) Developmental brain dynamics of numerical and arithmetic abilities. *npj Science of Learning 6*, 1, 22.

Books

Babtie, P. and Emerson, J. (2015) *Understanding Dyscalculia and Numeracy Difficulties: A Guide for Parents, Teachers and Other Professionals*. London: Jessica Kingsley Publishers.

Bird, R. (2017) *The Dyscalculia Resource Book: Games and Puzzles for 7 to 14*. SAGE Publications.

Butterworth, B. (2018) *Dyscalculia: From Science to Education*. Routledge.

Butterworth, B. and Yeo, D. (2014) *Dyscalculia Guidance: Helping Students with Specific Learning Difficulties in Maths*. NferNelson Publishing.

Chinn, S. (2012) *More Trouble with Maths*. Routledge.

Chinn, S. (2020) *How to Teach Maths: Understanding Learners Needs*. Routledge.

Eadle, C. and Chinn, S. (2023) *Succeed with Dyscalculia: Teaching Ideas and Worksheets for Learners with Maths Difficulties and Dyscalculia, Books 1–6*. SEN Books.

Eastaway, R. and Askew, M. (2010) *Maths for Mums and Dads: Take the Pain out of Homework*. Pavilion Publishing and Media.

Eastaway, R. and Askew, M. (2013) *More Maths for Mums and Dads: The Teenage Years*. Pavilion Publishing and Media.

Emerson, J. and Babtie, P. (2013) *The Dyscalculia Assessment*. Bloomsbury Education.

Emerson, J. and Babtie, P. (2014) *The Dyscalculia Solution: Teaching Number Sense*. Bloomsbury Education.

Hornigold, J. and Jewell, R. (2022) GCSE Maths for Neurodivergent Learners. London: Jessica Kingsley Publishers.

Jackson, L.M. (2022) *Discovering Dyscalculia: One Family's Journey with a Maths Disability*. GHF Press.

Presentations

Goring, J. (2023–24) Working towards a definition and guidance for Dyscalculia and Maths Difficulties. Dyscalculia and Maths Difficulties Working Group on behalf of SASC. www.sasc.org.uk/media/adiflafs/working-towards-a-definition-and-guidance-for-sasc-17-5-24.pdf

Jarrett, P. (2022) Dyscalculia as part of a bigger picture. A presentation for the British Dyslexia Association. https://cdn.bdadyslexia.org.uk/uploads/documents/About/APPG/Pete-Jarrett_Dyscalculia-as-part-of-a-bigger-picture.pdf?v=1671100952

Website

https://www.sasc.org.uk/media/3gtdmm0s/assessment-of-dyscalculia-maths-sasc-nov-2019.pdf

About the Authors

Jane Emerson

Jane Emerson trained as a speech and language therapist. During her training, she visited the St Bartholemew's Hospital Dyslexia Clinic, founded by Beve Hornsby. After qualifying, she worked with preschool children for the NHS and then with school-age students at the Dyslexia Teaching Centre, London. Later, she founded Emerson House, Centre for Dyslexic Primary Students. She was joined by the late Dorian Yeo who became Director of Numeracy and developed a new approach, inspired by Dr Steve Chinn, for the teaching of numeracy for students with dyspraxia and dyscalculia.

She developed Dorian Yeo's work for primary students with dyscalculia, and for several years ran training courses with Ronit Bird at Emerson House for local teachers. Jane wrote several books with Patricia Babtie, including *The Dyscalculia Assessment* and *The Dyscalculia Solution*, which were both published by Bloomsbury.

Jane worked alongside Robert Jennings at Emerson House, and they both realized that a formative assessment was necessary to identify those students who were having maths difficulties or dyscalculia in a relatively short time and where a teaching intervention plan could be formulated based on the analysis of student errors. The MDA stands as a unique assessment tool to inform students' needs accurately and usefully in order to help each student reach their potential in number-based maths.

Rob Jennings

Rob is the co-founder of the Dyscalculia Network, which provides training and advice for adults, educators and parents of students who may or may not have dyscalculia or maths difficulties.

He has over ten years of experience teaching young people with special educational needs. Over the past eight years, he has focused specifically on helping children struggling with maths, working in both independent and state schools.

In his role as Head of Maths at Emerson House LLP and Head of Learning Support at Westminster Abbey Choir School, Rob worked alongside educators and with parents to create and deliver personalized intervention plans for students.

Rob is a member of the British Psychological Society and has trained as a Certified Educational Assessor. He holds an OCR Level 5 Diploma in Teaching Learners with Specific Learning Difficulties (Distinction) from the Helen Arkell Training Centre, UK.

He is a member of the Crested Council and represents issues about dyscalculia and maths difficulties throughout specialist schools in the UK.

Rob presents across a number of educational exhibitions (TES Show in London, Dyslexia/Dyscalculia Show at the NEC, Birmingham, Toucan Educational Exhibition in Newcastle and FOBISIA (Federation of British Schools in Asia)). He is also engaged in teacher training in schools, further education colleges and adult education establishments.

NOTES

NOTES

NOTES

NOTES

NOTES

NOTES

NOTES

NOTES

NOTES

of related interest

GCSE Maths for Neurodivergent Learners
Build Your Confidence in Number, Proportion and Algebra
Judy Hornigold and Rose Jewell
Illustrated by Sophie Kennedy
Forewords by Steve Chinn and Charlie Stripp
ISBN 978 1 78775 700 4
eISBN 978 1 78775 701 1

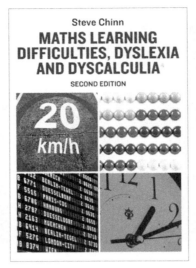

Maths Learning Difficulties, Dyslexia and Dyscalculia
Second Edition
Steve Chinn
ISBN 978 1 78592 579 5
eISBN 978 1 78450 989 7

Awesome Games and Activities for Kids with Numeracy Difficulties
How to Feel Smart and In Control about Doing Mathematics with a Neurodiverse Brain
Judy Hornigold
Illustrated by Joe Salerno
ISBN 978 1 78775 563 5
eISBN 978 1 78775 564 2